5/01

6.25

The R
Freedom

D0888956

by Jabari Asim

JAMESTOWN  PUBLISHERS

a division of NTC/CONTEMPORARY PUBLISHING GROUP
Lincolnwood, Illinois USA

For Liana and the children.

Cover Credits
   Design: Herman Adler Design Group
   Illustration: Douglass C. Klauba
   Timeline: (left) North Wind; (middle) Courtesy National Park Service;
      (right) North Wind

Photos
   Pages iii, 127, 129, 130, Library of Congress; pages 128, 131, Corbis

ISBN: 0-8092-0583-1 (hardbound)
ISBN: 0-8092-0625-0 (softbound)

Published by Jamestown Publishers,
a division of NTC/Contemporary Publishing Group, Inc.,
4255 West Touhy Avenue,
Lincolnwood (Chicago), Illinois 60712-1975 U.S.A.
© 2000 Jabari Asim

00 01 02 03 04 ML 10 9 8 7 6 5 4 3 2 1

An engraving including the Proclamation of Emancipation,
a portrait of Abraham Lincoln, and seven scenes depicting
slavery and plantation life.

Prologue

I'm an old man now, so old that from time to time my mind plays tricks on me and I forget that I've lived a long life and covered a lot of ground. Funny thing about memories: It's the things that happened yesterday that fade away first. The furthest-away times remain clear in my mind. Sometimes I feel that I could just reach out and touch the people I knew when I was just a boy, the men and women who took a liking to me and taught me valuable things.

For years I was a professor of English composition at Alabama's Tuskegee Normal and Industrial Institute, and I used to run my own newspaper too. As I sit at my desk near the open window and let the warm Alabama breeze gently drift across my face, I can easily recall those days when I worked side by side with those renowned scholars, the school's founder, Booker T. Washington and George

Washington Carver. Those were exciting times. It's my childhood days, though, that stand out the most. I can lean back in my chair, close my eyes, and watch the years melt away like ice in a glass of lemonade. I'm a child once more, and there's a war going on . . .

Chapter 1

Sometimes, when I think back on those first days of freedom, my memories begin with a loud bang. My mind returns to the old plantation in North Carolina, where one spring morning the sound of an explosion splits the air.

I hear the sound; then I see my massa falling from his saddle like in a dream, slowly sliding to the ground as Gray Bob rears up in fear. Massa Stewart lies still on the ground; and the horse, screaming, takes off into the fields.

Other times when I'm remembering, I don't hear the shot at all. Everything seems real quiet, frozen in silence as Massa falls and the horse's forelegs tilt up from the ground. Every time I think back, though, I recall Pa hollering to me across from the coop, where I'm gathering eggs.

"Ezra! Down! Down!" my Pa shouts at me, and I fall to the dirt. The egg basket bounces once, twice, then tumbles

over. Shells crack. Yolks ooze on the ground, yellow in the warming sun.

For a minute, all was still. Then I raised my head just a little and saw my father carefully making his way toward Massa, keeping low to the ground.

"Leave him be!"

A voice from the trees halted my father's approach.

We looked up and saw a Union officer riding toward us on a horse. Walking beside him was a young soldier. His uniform was torn, and he'd just about walked out of his boots. Behind those two, another soldier lurked, staring up into the woods. He appeared to be talking to a tree.

Pa looked at the officer. Then he looked at me. He didn't say anything, but his eyes told me to stay still.

We both looked at Massa Stewart. He was stretched out on his belly with his head turned to one side. His eyes were closed, but his mouth was wide open, as if he was trying to take a bite out of the earth. A dark red pool was slowly spreading beneath his jaw. He had moaned a little when he first fell, but now he was silent and completely still. Pa looked like he wanted to go to him.

"Whatever you thinkin', boy, you'd best put it out of your head," the officer said. "I don't plan to warn you again." The young soldier silently helped the officer from his horse. Once he was down, the officer bent over Massa and touched his neck. "Took a mouthful of dirt, this one," he said. "J.B., invite Logan and Crowder to join us."

The young soldier turned and waved his arm wildly

4

above his head. Seeing him, the one called Logan shouted something up into the tree branches above where he stood. Then an amazing thing happened. The tree moved and part of it took the shape of a man. Suddenly I could make him out against the background of the trunk as he shimmied down to the ground. I'd never seen a man like him. I was pretty sure that he was a white man, but his whole face was smeared with streaks of black and green, the dark bands so close together that none of his real color showed. He had leaves and twigs stuck to his cap and shoulders and mud all over his clothes. Bees circled and buzzed about his head, but he didn't even bother to swat at them. I could tell that he smelled something awful too, even with some distance still between us. He cradled his rifle gently, as if it were a baby. Anyone could tell, though, that it would take a whole regiment of rebs to tear that rifle from his hands.

The soldiers allowed us to get to our feet. I brushed myself off, and my pa came and stood by my side. I couldn't help staring at Crowder, the one who looked like a tree.

The officer grinned at us. "You boys like to dance?"

It was a strange question. My father looked at the officer but only for a second. Then he looked at the ground. "Don't feel much like dancing, suh," he replied. "Massa's dead."

The officer laughed and spat. He had a mustache like a thick brush, and his face was cracked and lined like old cowhide. "Your massa's been aiding the cause of the rebel army. He brought it on himself. Now listen here, if I was a darkie I would sure feel like dancing. Yes sir, I'd be steppin' lightly indeed if a sergeant in the United States Army came to me and told me he had something for me."

My Pa scratched his head and tried not to look at Massa stretched out on the ground. "I don't understand, suh. What did you bring us?"

The sergeant grinned again. "A little something called freedom," he said.

Some of Massa's slaves had already run off by the time Sergeant Dobson and his men arrived. Although Massa once had over 100 slaves, there couldn't have been more than 50 during our last days on the plantation—and more than a dozen of those were children. Pa said he stayed on because memories of my mother held him to the place, but I suspect he figured that it would be too hard to run and take me with him. I would have slowed him down with my bad foot and all.

From what I learned by talking to other folks, turns out Massa wasn't really so bad. I'm sure it's true what the sergeant said about him, but that don't make him evil through and through. Now his son, Judah, he was wicked as the Devil himself. Everybody tried to stay out of his way until he took off to fight for the rebs. Judah died in his first skirmish, and old Massa was never the same after that. He sent Missus to stay with her people and keep out of harm's way.

Missus came from a fine family in Virginia. She was very dainty and fond of dressing up in pretty clothes.

Many times she took pity on us little children and would let Clara, her cook, feed us in the yard near the big house. The delicious smell of bread would ride the air from the kitchen, where Clara sweated over an old brick fireplace. Until I got old enough to work for John the yardman, helping him make barrels and furniture and the like, I'd answer the Missus's call and gather 'round with my friends. Clara would hand out johnnycake fresh from her great big skillet—and gourds of buttermilk to wash it down. I remember pulling the soft, warm cake to my mouth, licking the rich crumbs from my fingers. When Missus went back to her folks, those treats ended, and so did many of the routines around the farm. Massa took to spending a lot of time in town, and he trusted Pa and Luke, the other foreman, to keep things going when he wasn't around. I filled in whenever and wherever I could, doing everything from pulling weeds to gathering eggs.

Massa's main money crops were cotton, tobacco, and indigo, but we raised plenty of peas, chickens, eggs, cows, and pigs besides. Sometimes it seemed that Massa didn't care as much about his crops as he once did, or about anything else for that matter. But work got done all the same. After all, we all depended on the success of the crops. We did a lot for ourselves, though. The slave women made most of our clothes by carding, spinning, and weaving cloth from the cotton. Then they'd dye it from mixtures made of bark and leaves and make shirts, dresses, and pants. Most boys didn't wear pants until they got pretty big. They ran around in shirttails, although I didn't because Emma made me pants. Emma was a big, friendly-faced slave who was especially good at sewing. My Pa would do chores for her in exchange for her kindness. While we heard a lot about some slaves having to survive winter in their bare feet, we had no such problems. Emma and the other women knitted stockings, and we had shoes on top of that. Massa had taught my Pa, Luke, John, and some of the other men how to make brogans from cowhide. First they slaughtered the cow and tanned its hide by soaking it in oak ashes and water, then cut a pattern from the leather.

Pa and I had our own log cabin. There were some two-room cabins in the quarters, but ours was just one room. Everybody slept on pallets stuffed with straw and hay and shucks. Even after folks started running off, people tried to keep things nice. We made brooms from sage and kept our dirt floors neatly swept. Pa and I didn't have much in our little place, and we had even less after the soldiers helped themselves.

More soldiers came soon after Sergeant Dobson. They were a rowdy bunch, full of spit and vinegar and not nearly as worn down as Dobson's little crew. They rooted and looted up and down the quarters, taking what little food and treasures we'd set aside, tearing up our pallets in search of coins and whatnot. They even took the pine knots and flint rocks that we used to light our way to the fields. Worst of all for me and Pa was when they took my mama's dress. Pa had kept it for as long as I could remember. Sometimes at night when he thought I was asleep, he'd hold my mama's dress and talk as if she was still in it. It was little more than a faded rag, but I knew he felt awful bad when that soldier snatched it up. I felt bad too, and I couldn't even remember my mama.

The soldiers had made us stand aside while they tore up our place. My father took a step forward as if he meant to take the dress from the soldier's hands. A rifle stopped him. "Out of the way, now," said the soldier holding it. He didn't cock his piece, but he pressed it into my father's belly. "Unless you want a rifle ball in your gut."

"This is right pretty," he continued. He was surprisingly heavy as soldiers went. Most of his fellow soldiers were bony and hard. "Bet the gal who fills it is right nice too."

"She is," my father said, forgetting himself. "Was."

The fat soldier looked up, rubbing the dress against his whiskers. "Was?"

Pa looked away. "She's gone," he said. "Don't know where."

"Well, if she's gone, then it ain't no use to her now, is it?"

When Pa didn't answer, the man stuffed the dress into his sack. "Maybe I'll carry it into battle. Might bring me luck against them dirty rebs."

I could see the muscles in my father's jaw working. They rippled beneath the skin of his face as he struggled to keep his feelings inside. He didn't breathe another word until the men had left our cabin.

When they were done with the quarters, the Yankees

tore up most of the big house in search of silverware, jewelry, fine cloth—whatever they could get their hands on, although, to my surprise, they didn't find much. Then they camped out in the rubble they'd made.

That night they held a big party and made all of us come. We wanted to celebrate, sure, but right then we were more worried than happy. After all, Sergeant Dobson and his men had said they were bringing us freedom, but they hadn't told us that we were free to go. In fact, that afternoon, they'd set us to work gathering vegetables from the fields, repairing their wagons and seeing to their horses. They made the house servants heat water for their baths and attend to their toilets, and they made poor Clara cook for hours on end, preparing a feast of hot biscuits, coffee, sweet potatoes, roast chicken, and greens. The soldiers were rough and ready, and when we dared to ask what would become of us, they just whooped and hollered and kept carrying on.

Rufus had been summoned to find a couple of fiddles. He was an old hand who had played for all the plantation dances. He played for us at our frolics too, or on Sundays after we had religion, and in the quarters when we had celebrations of our own. Because Massa never let our people marry for real like white folks did, couples who fell in love just jumped the broom. An old hand would say a few words, the couple would jump over a broom handle, he would say, "That's your wife." Then the playing and dancing would commence. Times like that, when everybody was filled with gladness, so happy that we

10

almost forgot we were slaves, it seemed like Rufus could make a fiddle talk. When he got to sawing that bow across the strings, he'd throw back his head and begin to sing.

Fool my Massa seven years.
Going to fool him seven more.
Hey diddle, de diddle, de diddle, de do.

For the white folks, Rufus played the reels that Missus liked, and old-time songs like "Jimmy Long Josey" and "Black-Eye Susie." I'd always thought that Rufus was the best fiddler anywhere until I heard Crowder.

Like the other men, he'd cleaned himself up. He'd scrubbed all the coal from his face, combed the twigs and leaves from his dark hair and slicked it into place. A body could get close enough to get a good look at him, if one dared. I thought he was fascinating—here was a man who could turn himself into a tree, fade into the woods as if he never been standing there at all—and then, with a little tallow soap, turn himself into flesh and blood again. He stood out though, even among the other soldiers. There was something in his eyes that was hard to figure, a queer expression. Even though I was just 10, I knew in my bones that Mr. Crowder was a man who could just as easily kill you as lend you a lifesaving hand, depending on how he felt.

The other Yankees knew it too. They all kept a distance between themselves and Crowder, as if he was a disease they didn't want to catch. They all feared him and even despised him because they thought he was the worst kind of soldier: a marksman—a sniper who hid in trees and caught Confederate soldiers unawares. Amid the drinking and carousing I heard soldiers mutter words like "assassin" and "coward" and "dishonor." But none of them said a thing to his face.

The soldiers took turns dancing with the prettiest of our women, squeezing them tightly and whirling them around and around until they were out of breath. Then, before the women could rest for a minute, other soldiers would come and take them in their arms.

Crowder took the lead and played the most beautiful music I'd ever heard, sweet and sorrowful and haunting all at once. At first, Rufus was confused and couldn't follow. After a while he caught on, and the two men smiled at each other, their fiddles talking and sighing back and forth as they spun a wonderful web of sound.

Pa and I watched as more of our people began to join in, dancing among themselves, away from the soldiers but still close enough to hear the music. They swayed and turned and stepped and skipped. The moonlight and the glow of the bonfire blazing in the crisp spring air chased away their fears and suspicions.

Soon we found ourselves near Logan and J.B., the men who'd come with Dobson and Crowder. Logan sat on the ground with a bottle of whiskey in one hand, a half-eaten drumstick in the other. His legs were splayed, and his back was pressed against the trunk of a tree. J.B. stood next to him, staring in the direction of the party but looking far beyond it, as if he was gazing into a window to another world, or maybe his own memories.

The two men seemed to understand each other. They'd worked out a system where Logan did the talking, and J.B. just grunted or nodded. Logan rubbed his eye with his fist, the drumstick drawing small circles in the air. Then he turned to my father. "You wondering how come this youngster's so quiet?

"He's seen too much," he said before Pa could answer.

"Seen too much, suh?"

I could tell that Pa was as curious as I was.

"That's what I said," Logan continued. "It was dead children. Dead white children." He turned his bottle up to his mouth and took a long swallow. Some of the whiskey spilled on his whiskers, but he didn't seem to mind.

"I'm a cook, see? Sam Logan cooks, J.B. assists, and Sergeant Dobson commands. We work with that devil, Mr. Crowder. He turns himself into a tree or a bush or a haystack or a snake in the grass, takes down a reb with his Sharps; then we come clean up the mess he's made. We protect him, escort him so that he can do his dirty work." Sam Logan belched.

"J.B., being the loyal private he is, is walking watch around a little abandoned town we found in our meanderings. Just a few houses, the people are gone, and so we're camping there for the night. A most dutiful sentry, that J.B. Here's to you, friend."

Logan raised his bottle in a toast. He waved the bottle in Pa's direction. Surprised, Pa just shook his head. J.B. stood and stared.

"He come across something in a shed. Something caught his eye, interrupted his patrol. I don't know, a glint of light, the squeak of a rat—something. Took a look in a window and shouted, which is the last thing you want to do when you're walking watch. Shouted long and loud, didn't you, buddy? Woke us up and we come running, armed to the teeth. I'm a cook, see, but I know my way around a rifle.

"The shed's full of dead children, all shot. Couldn't find hide nor hair of their mamas and papas, and didn't have time to look. We had to make hay on account of J.B.'s shouting. He's seen too much, see. Been shut up like a barn door ever since."

Logan turned on us and we never saw it coming. "Dead white children, understand? Babies murdered, fine youngsters gone all quiet, our country's best men shedding blood so you coloreds can be free."

Logan was shouting now, his voice nearly as loud as the music. We wondered if anyone else could hear him. J.B. just stared. "White men are paying a price for you, see. Your freedom ain't free. Somebody's got to pay for it, understand? Of course you don't, you stupid, black brute!"

Logan was suddenly standing. He smashed his bottle against the tree behind him and thrust the jagged handle at Pa and me. Pa put one strong arm in front of me.

"One step backward, Ezra," my father said softly, never taking his eyes off Logan. "Then another. One step at a time." He opened his palm toward Logan. "We don't want no trouble, suh," my father said loudly.

14

Logan raised his weapon a little higher. "Ha! That's all you people are. Trouble!"

Pa and I heard something whistle past our ears. A knife shredded Logan's sleeve and pinned his arm to the tree trunk. Stunned, he turned and looked. His arm was untouched.

Behind us, the music had stopped. Everyone stared in shocked silence at Mr. Crowder, who had expertly pulled and tossed his knife with one hand, without dropping the fiddle and bow he cradled carefully in the other.

"He's the Devil, see?" Logan shouted and struggled to free himself from the tree. "None but the Devil himself could move so fast!"

"Stop your muttering, you drunken fool," Sergeant Dobson commanded. "You sound like one of these superstitious darkies." He turned to my father.

"You, there. What did you say to my soldier?"

"I don't rightly know, suh," my father said. "I thought he was offering me a drink, but next thing I know he's waving a broken bottle at me and my boy."

"He lies!" Logan, unable to pull the knife from the tree, had ripped his sleeve to escape. The blue flap fluttered against the trunk like a scrap of flag. "He tried to take my whiskey," Logan charged.

"I saw the whole thing, Sergeant," Crowder said. His voice was low and calm, with just a hint of danger in it. "The black man speaks the truth. Logan was threatening him, and the black man had no weapon. It was a dishonorable situation."

The sergeant looked at Crowder, amused.
"Dishonorable?" Dobson moved close to the marksman, as if to prove that, unlike the other soldiers, he wasn't afraid. "Strange talk coming from one who sneaks up on his enemies and shoots them in the back."

Crowder smiled. His teeth seemed too incredibly white to belong to a man who spent most of his time skulking around in the woods and crawling through muddy fields. "I only shoot when you give the order, Sergeant," he replied.

The men glared at each other for what seemed like forever before Sergeant Dobson gave up and turned away. "That's it, folks," he shouted. "Party's over! It's getting late, and we've got a lot of work ahead of us. Go on back to the quarters. We'll summon you in the morning."

The Union soldiers, grumbling and stumbling, moved to obey the sergeant's order. Having stuffed themselves on Clara's lip-smacking victuals and swallowed much of our dead Massa's good whiskey, they shuffled toward the mansion, wearing the smiles of the deeply satisfied. Luke and John hurried to put out the fire while Clara and a few others prepared to store away what was left of the food. Sergeant Dobson stopped my father. He jabbed a finger sharply into Pa's chest.

"You better watch yourself, boy," he warned. "I'm keeping an eye on you."

"Yes, suh," Pa answered.

The sergeant walked away.

"So, Pa," I said looking up at him. "Are we really free?"

Pa reached down and lifted me onto his shoulders. He seemed to always know when my foot was causing me pain. Up above me the heavens were filled with more stars than I'd seen in a long time. They twinkled and glowed against a deep black sky.

"I suspect not, son. I believe that when we're really, truly free, somehow we'll know it."

Chapter 2

Back in our cabin, Pa and I each took a shirt and rolled up the rest of our clothes inside it. Then we pulled the sleeves and tied them together, making each bundle into a kind of knapsack. We used our bundles as pillows as we curled up on the dirt floor to sleep. Our pallets, slit up and torn apart, were of little use anymore.

I found it hard to sleep, and not just because of the hard ground beneath me. The full moon shone through the cracks in the cabin, and outside every living critter tried to make itself heard. The lonely crickets sang their mating songs in the tall grass, hounds howled at the far-off stars—I even thought I could hear the bass jumping in the creek. I heard muffled voices coming from cabins up and down the quarters: whispered, heartfelt prayers; excited laughter; occasional sobs. I had never recollected a night so loud and so bright. Now I realize that I was simply trying to remember everything, to press into my brain every single detail of my last night on the Stewart plantation. My last night in the slave quarters. I rolled over onto my back and stared up through the seams in the logs. I wondered if there were people on the moon and if some of them were slaves too. I wondered about my mother, whether she was alive as Pa always said, if I would ever see her.

I'd never been off the plantation before, and I wondered about that too. How big was the world? Was it busy and noisy and crowded with people? Was life out there any more dangerous than being a slave? I could hear Pa tossing and turning. From time to time he'd let out a long sigh. I knew he was puzzling over riddles of his own.

Finally I broke the silence between us.

"Pa?"

"Yeah, son?"

I knew my father had to grow tired of the questions I'd thrown at him all my life. I knew he often wished he had someone else there to share in my upbringing. All the same, I couldn't help being curious. I used to look in on Emma a lot, asking her how clothes were made, how she made the dyes that changed the color of cloth. Once I even asked her if she knew how to make black folks turn white. She never expressed impatience toward me, even when she didn't have an answer. She told me being curious was in my nature. And of course she was right.

"About my mother, Pa—"

"She's out there, son. If Journee was dead—if she wasn't out there I'd know. I'd feel it."

"She's been gone so long."

Pa sighed again. We'd had this conversation before. "It's only been eight years, Ezra. I know that seems like a long time to a young 'un like you, but really it ain't. In God's time that ain't no time at all."

I wanted to say that God sure was taking his sweet time bringing her back to us, but I knew better.

"You think she'll know me?"

"A mother always knows her child, Ezra. You can be sure of that."

"Emma says the same thing," I said. "She hasn't seen her son since he was sold away thirty-five years ago. She says she'd recognize him right away if he walked through her cabin door."

I knew my father was grinning even though I wasn't looking at him. He liked that kind of talk. "You should listen to that woman, I tell you. She knows what she's talking about," he said.

I propped up on one elbow and looked across at my father. I saw his strong, handsome profile, how even at rest he seemed alert, powerful. How such a mighty man could have a weak, crippled son like me was a constant puzzle to me. "Pa? Do you ever wish you had a son who was more like you?"

"I already have a son like me. His name's Ezra Taplin. You know him?"

"Come on, Pa. I'm serious. I mean a boy with a

healthy foot who doesn't get tired so quick. The two of you could have run by now, gone all the way to Canada."

"Healthy foot, crippled foot, no foot at all—I wasn't going to run anywhere with anybody without hearing something about Journee. Where she is, where she'd been seen, anything. God gave you to me, Ezra. You the boy I'm supposed to have, and I'm glad about it. Everybody running off to freedom and what do you know? Freedom came to us."

We were both quiet for awhile, absorbing the night sounds all around us.

"Pa?" I said.

"Hmm?"

"When Mr. Crowder shot Massa, do you think Missus felt it all the way in Virginia?"

"I bet she did, son. When the Sergeant let Luke and me bury Massa, I said a prayer for Missus too."

The dawn was misty and bone-chilling cold. Heavy gray clouds hung just above our heads. It was hard to see our hands in front of our faces. We loaded the Union wagons with supplies and horse feed while Clara and her helpers, still weary from yesterday's labors, cooked up enough food to last all day. Sergeant Dobson told us we were headed to a Union camp on Roanoke Island. He said we'd make it in three days if we covered about 20 miles each day. Once we arrived there we'd be left in the custody of the troops. Dobson would join J.B., Logan, and Crowder, who'd gone ahead. There'd be no tarrying, he warned. The old people and children would have to keep up. We were taking Massa's cows with us, and they'd have to be managed carefully. After we helped with the morning's chores, Pa and I slung our "knapsacks" onto sticks and went to join the others. By now a light rain was falling.

Marcus, one of our young men, around 20, stood in front of Dobson with his arms folded in front of him. Marcus looked angry. Dobson looked amused.

"If I didn't know any better," the sergeant was saying. "I'd think you were looking me straight in the eye. But it is right foggy out here. Can make things appear to be what they ain't."

Marcus scowled. "Might seem like I'm looking at you, but I'm looking at Arkansas. I got people in Arkansas, and I figure that's where I should be headed."

"This fog makes it hard to see for sure," said the sergeant, "but it shouldn't make it hard to hear. I said we're headed to Roanoke Island. I didn't say a durn thing about no Arkansas."

"Yesterday you tell me I got freedom. Today you tell me I got to go where you say."

I could see Dobson getting impatient. He began to rub the handle of his sword like it had an itch that needed scratching. "You're free, all right," he said. "But you ain't white. And until you are, you'd best do what a white man tells you."

Most of us were trying not to study the situation too much. Marcus was saying what we all were thinking but didn't let on. Best to let Marcus do all the talking right now. The soldiers, on the other hand, were ready to roll on. They'd had their fill of the plantation's offerings and were looking ahead to future treasures, I suppose.

"Come on, Sarge! The fog is lifting," one of them shouted.

"Yeah, Sarge," another called. "Can we get to marching?"

Suddenly Marcus sat down in the road. He looked up at Dobson, defiant. "I don't know nothin' about Roanoke. I ain't going."

"You're right about that," the Sarge said quickly. He pulled out his pistol and shot Marcus in the chest. He fell down dead, his eyes wide open.

We'd all seen plenty of death. We knew enough not to cry out or protest around the whites who had us in their power. Sometimes just the show of emotion was cause enough to bring more death on our heads, so we just bore our sadness quietly, our faces tight masks until we were alone and could properly mourn our departed. We all stared at Marcus as if committing him to memory, watching the chilly rain fall into his open, unseeing eyes.

Dobson turned to us, his mouth firm. "Anybody else got any questions? Good. Men! Let's move 'em out!"

About five miles into the woods we heard shouts from Dobson's scouts. In time we found them circling excitedly around a pile of brush. Soon the other soldiers joined them and began to clear away the brush. It was hard to see exactly what was going on. When we got closer we saw that they had uncovered two big wooden doors laying flat to the ground. After some grunting and struggling they managed to open them. The opening led to a huge pit in the earth, deeper and wider than Massa's smokehouse. It was filled with chinaware and silver, fine cloth, even money—everything that the soldiers had been unable to find at the big house.

My father and Luke and a couple of the stronger hands were called upon to use a rope ladder to descend into the pit. The soldiers watched intently as each trunk and basket was hauled to the surface. Then they quickly grabbed it and loaded it aboard for the rest of our journey. By the time they were done, the wagons were nearly sagging under the weight of all the added goods. I didn't envy the horses at all.

We thought Sergeant Dobson was about to give the order to roll out, but instead he paused, looking up and down our line as if searching for someone. His eyes rested on Pa and Luke.

"You two! Get over here! Now!"

Pa and Luke exchanged looks, then went to face the sergeant. While my father was a tall man, Luke was even taller. He was so dark that his skin had a bluish tint, and although not as thickly built as Pa, he looked strong just the same. His long, wiry arms were knotted with strips of tough muscle. He was a quiet, easygoing man who could work for long hours in the field without tiring, often softly humming a mysterious tune as he moved from row to row.

Dobson looked like he was hankering to hit them. "The two of you were Stewart's foremen?"

"That's right, suh," my father replied.

"That means he trusted ya, as far as you can trust a slave, I mean. Ain't that right?"

"I reckon, suh," Luke said.

The sergeant grinned, but he didn't look friendly at all. More like a wolf baring his fangs. "Well he sure knew how to pick 'em. You watched us tear up that mansion looking for goods, and you didn't say a mumbling word. And you were gonna let us walk right by this hideaway if my men hadn't discovered it. Ain't that right?"

Dobson took out his pistol.

"Not our place to tell white men's secrets, suh," Pa said, his eyes on Dobson's gun.

"Not your place! It's not your place to decide your place! That's up to me! I'll tell you what your place is!" Dobson was breathing hard, and his face was red as flame. His mustache shook as he spoke.

He turned to Luke, who didn't seem to know what the fuss was about. "And you," said Dobson, "why didn't you tell us?"

"You didn't ask, suh."

Dobson snarled and swung his gun, a heavy Navy Colt. He smashed the butt of it against Luke's nose, and Luke sank to his knees. Blood shot out of Luke's face like a fountain and spurted onto his shirt. Luke's wife, Tempie, screamed. Emma stretched forth her big arms and wrapped Tempie in them. Another woman grabbed Mary, Luke's daughter, and pulled her face to her bosom. My pa took a step backward, his palms raised in front of him.

Dobson must have forgotten about him while dealing with Luke, because he looked at my father as if noticing him for the first time. "I'm tired of looking up at you," he said sternly. His voice was softer now. "Get on your knees."

Pa knelt beside Luke, who was gently rocking back and forth. Luke began to hum his tune, a little louder than unusual. The song reminded me of a prayer, though it had no words.

I closed my eyes for just a moment, and a picture of Marcus formed inside my head. He was still dead, still stretched out in the road as the wagon ruts filled up with rain. I opened my eyes and saw Pa looking at me. He looked as though he'd given up, as though he was prepared to die. His sad eyes were full of regret, as if he felt bad about having to leave me all alone. We were just five miles from the plantation, farther than I'd been in my life. Too far, I thought. I wished right then that we were back in the fields, that Massa was still astride Gray Bob, that everything was like it was before Crowder shimmied up that tree.

"You're both guilty of treason," Dobson said. "Treason in wartime is punishable by death." He cocked his pistol.

"Wait a minute, Sarge," a voice called from the front of our little procession. He stepped forward. It was the fat soldier who'd taken my mother's dress.

"Maybe we should think this through," he suggested.

"What's to think?" Dobson asked, still staring at Pa and Luke. "These coloreds are still loyal to their master, a stinking reb. They're traitors to the Union's cause."

"They're not even citizens, Sarge," the fat man said. "Only citizens can commit treason. I guess right now all you can say is these men are property of the federal government. Maybe it's best that we just turn them over to the authorities when we get to camp."

"I was planning to do that anyway," said the sergeant, annoyed. "Are you a lawyer, Private?"

The fat man reddened, then smiled. "Yes sir, as a matter of fact I am."

Dobson uncocked his gun and holstered it. He rubbed his temples with both hands. "Lawyers in the army," he sighed. "A sure sign that the end is near. You two get out of my sight, before I change my mind and kill you anyway."

Before I knew it I was hugging Pa and laughing and crying at the same time. The fat soldier interrupted us. He had something for Pa. "Here," he said, handing over my mother's dress. "I just missed stepping on a rattler a while back. Figured I'd better spread some of that luck around."

"I much obliged to ya, suh," Pa said. "Thank ya kindly."

The "authorities" on Roanoke Island were Horace James, the superintendent, and Holland Streeter, his assistant. I was riding atop Pa's shoulders when we staggered into camp. We were still woozy from the boat, which we had ridden from nearby Newbern. There were other groups of newcomers there as well. Mr. Streeter explained to us that each family would be given material to build their own cabin and an acre of ground to cultivate. In return for the government's kindness, the able-bodied men and women were expected to labor on the Union's behalf. In addition, the men would be paid 10 dollars a month.

I stood with Pa as he waited in line to register. Another black man, small and quick with laughing eyes, walked up and introduced himself. "Hiram Larkin," he said with a smile.

"Silas Taplin. And this here's my boy, Ezra." Pa and the man shook hands.

Pa asked Hiram how long he'd been on the island.

"About nine months," he said, shielding his eyes from the sun. "I haul stuff for the army. Lots of soldiers on this island, and plenty of 'em guardin' this camp. They'll have plenty for you to do."

"I've worked all my life," Pa said. "Lord knows I can handle work, and getting paid besides just makes it all the sweeter."

Hiram looked curiously at my father. "Paid, huh? Tell me somethin'. When you was bustin' your back for your massa, did you ever think about bein' free?"

"Sure," Pa replied. "I prayed on it often, and I wished for it more times than I could ever count."

Hiram grinned. "Is that right? Well, be careful what you wish for." He started laughing so much that he lost control of himself. "See ya 'round," he gasped between fits of laughter.

"What was that about, Pa?"

"I don't rightly know, son. And I'm not sure I want to."

That night we found out that not everyone in the crowded camp had been "liberated" as we had. Some of the people were relatives of black men fighting in the Union army. Not day laborers or grave diggers. Real soldiers. We learned all this from Mose Bolton, an old black man with a thick mane of hair that looked like cotton. We took our first meal at the Bolton's.

"My son James is with the First South," he explained on the way to his cabin.

I wasn't sure what he meant. "What's that, suh?"

"The First South Carolina Volunteer Infantry," he answered proudly.

Mose's family treated us like long-lost friends. "Mother," he called as he rapped on his front door. "We've got guests."

"Mother" was his wife, Fannie. She was a short, beaming round-faced woman of small, dainty movements. "How do?" she said warmly.

"This here's Silas Taplin and his boy, Ezra. I told them we had room at our table."

Fannie smiled. "Most of what we got is stuff I put up over the summer. Pole beans and pickled corn. Cornbread and molasses too."

My father bowed deeply. "We'd be much obliged, ma'am, for anything you don't mind sharing." We'd nearly starved on the way to camp. Dobson had fed the cows better than he'd fed us.

Mrs. Bolton excused herself and returned to her brick fireplace behind the cabin. The place was bigger than any cabin I'd ever seen. It had three good-sized rooms and a thatch window in the back wall. We'd learn later that an outhouse wasn't far away, and a brisk stride would take you to the well just inside a minute.

Mose watched as Pa and I gaped at our impressive new surroundings. "My grandson and I built this place," he said. "We built an extra room for visitors, meetings, and the like. Roanoke's the kind of place where people are always moving in and out. Folks find out where their family is; then they try to go to them."

Pa told Mr. Bolton about my mother and his intention to find her. Mr. Bolton nodded sympathetically but didn't say anything. After a while he retrieved his corncob pipe and lighted it. He nodded at Pa. "You smoke, Silas?"

Pa shook his head. "I reckon not, Mr. Bolton."

"You're a smart man, Silas. And call me Mose."

The rest of the Boltons showed up just before supper. Mose's daughter-in-law was named Ruth. She was a tall, slender woman, and although she was pleasant enough, she wasn't in the habit of smiling. Best of all, she had two children. Cinda was 11 (and, I couldn't help noticing, very beautiful) and Paul was 13. We made acquaintance while we ate and shamelessly listened in on the adults' conversation.

"If you don't get something in the ground right away you'll be dependent on the government's rations," Fannie said. "Sometimes they're late, and sometimes they don't come at all."

30

"Lots of people don't eat every day so they can stretch their victuals out," Mose joined in. "The winter was hard. We all shared, but it wasn't enough. Some of us didn't make it."

"Be careful what you wish for," Pa said.

Mose leaned forward, his elbows on the table. "What's that?"

My father looked suddenly ashamed. "Oh, I was just thinking of something a fellow said to me. Hiram Larkin."

Mose chuckled. His wife sucked her teeth in disgust. Ruth rolled her eyes. "You could do better than to listen to that lazy bum," Mose said. "Some black folk want to be back in slavery because they crave the routine. They can't stand the random confusion that freedom brings. They have to think for themselves for the very first time. Some folks don't like having to think. Hiram's one of them."

"I got no problem with thinking," Pa said. "Yet I can't help wondering why the government took us off the plantations just to set us down in another kind of plantation."

Mose smiled at Fannie. "You got to get up early in the morning to fool this man, Mother. Silas, my family and I are already quite used to our government's deceitful ways. Ain't much logic to them, far as I can see.

"We lost a lot to Union soldiers, understand. That's how we ended up here."

"I tried to hide things," Fannie recalled. "When the soldiers come to liberate us I tried to hide things. But they found them."

Mose filled in part of the story. "Our boy James had already run off to fight for the Union. Fannie and me thought it was a good thing for him to do. We kept an eye on his family. I had hired myself out as a carpenter for many years, and my massa allowed me to keep some things for Fannie and me on account I was valuable to him."

"But he never let Mose buy his freedom," Fannie said. "And when the Union came to give him his freedom, they took the bacon from under the house, the corn from the crib, the flour, and the lard. Some of the chickens they shot, and some they ran down."

Mose reached out and tenderly rubbed his wife's shoulders, which had tightened visibly as she talked. "All in all," he said, "they took twenty chickens, four or five bushels of cornmeal, half a barrel of lard, tubs, kettles, and a silk dress my missus had given Fannie long ago."

"And my son a Volunteer," Fannie said. "I told them we'd starve, but they said don't worry, that we'd get it all back again."

Mose got up and began to clear dishes from the table. "I submitted a claim for two hundred fifty dollars to the federal government," he said. "I got a hundred and ten dollars, which, thank the Lord, has given us an easier time than many of our people here."

The Boltons eventually offered us their guest room. They said we could stay there until Pa could save enough money for some building materials. We gratefully accepted, and Pa thanked God for our good fortune. In camp less than a day and already we'd made friends. Exhausted, we collapsed onto our new pallets and fell into deep sleep right away. The last sounds we heard were the Boltons' bittersweet harmonies, soft, sorrowful voices rising and fading in hushed tones.

Didn't my Lord deliver Daniel,
Deliver Daniel,
Deliver Daniel?
Didn't my Lord deliver Daniel?
Then why not every man?

Chapter 3

Some people had been living in the Union camp for more than two years, but Pa and I stayed little more than a month, not even long enough to build our own cabin. Outside Roanoke, battles near and far raged on. But they had little direct effect on our lives, reaching us only as rumors and vague whispers like the lightest of breezes. Pa started working right away, joining a crew that was building livestock pens for the army's growing herds. I joined Paul and Cinda on a trash gang, raking stubble and pulling weeds. Back on the plantation, the trash gang was made up almost entirely of women and slaves like me, who for one reason or another couldn't work in the fields for long stretches at a time: old people, women with nursing babies, and a few young people who were sick. In camp, our crew was made up almost entirely of young girls like Cinda. Paul and I were the only boys. Women found work as laundresses or cooks, or they tried to scratch out a garden in the camp's crusty soil.

Before freedom and before Massa's attention began to wander, I'd also toted water and tended livestock. I worked hard, but I also played hard. The other children and I played "You Can Catch Me," marbles, and smut (a game played with grains of corn). We hunted in the woods for grapes and berries. We played in the camp too, and sometimes we just sat around to swap lies and tell conjure stories. Paul knew more tales about hants, or ghosts, than anybody else in camp. We were all raised up Christian, and knew we had no business talking like that, but we did it just the same.

Late one afternoon I was sitting with Cinda, Paul, and a girl named Katie. Paul told us a fib about a phantom rider. "I heard a man named Matthew say he was riding home one night and a woman stepped out in the road and say, 'Matthew, let me ride.' He say, 'My hoss won't tote double.' She say, 'Yes, it will,' and she jump up behind him, and that hoss bucked and jumped nigh 'bout from under him, but when he got home, she wa'n't there. He say his sister had just died and it mighta been her."

Suddenly Paul froze up. His eyes rolled back in his head. I expected him to make a spooky, woo-woo sound, to try to scare us. But instead he just fell on the ground and began to flop like a fish out of water. Cinda leaned over him and began to fan his face. "It's okay, Paul," she said loudly. Then, without looking over at Katie, she spoke softly to her. "What's he doing?"

Katie slyly looked over my shoulder. I turned around and saw a Union soldier staring intently at us. "He's still looking," Katie whispered.

"What's wrong with him?" I asked, but no one answered my question. Katie kept eyeing the soldier, and Cinda kept fanning Paul. The strange scene ended after a couple of minutes when the soldier went on his way. Paul sat up and brushed off his shirt. He seemed to be fine.

"Is anybody gon' tell me what's going on?" I asked.

"They'll try to take him to Newbern," said Katie.

I learned that Newbern, North Carolina, was the home of a large plantation that was worked mainly by children—the children of the men and women living on Roanoke. Against their parents' wishes, these kids had been "conscripted" into service for the Union Army. After so many conscriptions, Paul was the only able-bodied boy left on Roanoke. He had managed to avoid being sent to Newbern by pretending to suffer from a strange and mysterious illness. That was why he started flopping like a fish when the Union soldier came near.

That night, Mose Bolton held a Bible talk at his cabin. He didn't actually have a Bible, but he spoke on things he remembered from religious meetings he'd attended as a slave. Then we all prayed for an end to the war and for true freedom. When Mose asked God to help us find our missing loved ones, Pa said "amen" louder than everyone else. In addition to Mose's family, there was Pa and me and about 10 other people, all men. Folks lingered after prayers to talk. Cinda had told Mose about Paul's close call, and Mose recounted the story to the people on hand.

"At least you still got Paul," said a man named Zeb. He carried a battered hat, which he twisted and pulled on as he spoke. "Simon ain't seen his boy in almost a year. Don't know if he's dead or alive."

"Our children ain't nothin' but slaves in Newbern," muttered a tall, tan-skinned fellow named Andy. "My boy and I used to wonder what freedom was like. Then the Union soldiers came through and took us with them. I didn't think it would be like this."

"I didn't wait for no soldiers," a deep, gravelly voice said. The voice belonged to a man who'd said little all evening. He was a medium-sized man, but he looked very strong. His name was Jasper, and the corners of his mouth hung down so far it looked as if he'd never smiled in his life. He spoke softly, but something about his voice and his expression kept us quiet and encouraged us to pay close attention.

"My massa joined the rebs," he said, and when he said "massa," it sounded like the worst insult in the world. "He put another white man over us. Man named Anderson. First thing he do is cut the rations. Three pounds of meat for the week, a peck of meal. We half starvin', but he want more work out of us. Work. Whippin'. Work. That's all we know. I got scars on my arms and back that I'll wear to my grave. I didn't wait for no Army. I run. I run till I find the Yanks' camp. They put me on a freight train with some other runaways—then they put me to work. I've built breastworks in Alabama and toted water in Tennessee.

I'm still bein' cheated out of rations, and I'm still waitin' on my pay. If I had someplace to run, I'd run again. But ain't nowhere to go."

Jasper's words stayed with me, echoing in my ears when I tried to sleep that night. They blended with Paul's hant story, and I found myself dreaming I was on the back of a horse. The phantom rider was a Union soldier. I couldn't get off the horse because it was moving too fast. I knew the soldier was taking me to Newbern. The phantom rider turned and laughed when I asked him to release me. All the skin on his face was gone, revealing a frightening skull underneath. I could see worms wriggling in and out of his eye sockets. "Let you go?" he howled. "Go where? Ain't nowhere to go." He cackled and urged his horse on. I woke up in a cold sweat, lying there for a long time until I imagined my mama singing me to sleep. I had no more dreams for the rest of the night.

Word of mouth was the way we communicated. Information was whispered from row to row until the entire plantation had been informed. Of course, sometimes the information was wrong or had been mysteriously changed by the time it made its way around. Sometimes it was hard to tell just what to believe. Still, the word *surrender* was passed about with some regularity on Roanoke. Our men watched the soldiers closely for any sign that victory was close at hand.

"It won't be a day too soon," Mose declared when Pa asked him about surrender. "We've lost so many men," he said, lighting up his pipe. "And I'm not just talking about buckras neither." "Buckras" was our name for white men, though sometimes we called them "patrollers." The Confederates we sometimes called "secesh" because they were trying to secede from the Union.

Mose seemed to know lots more than we did about the war. He preferred to talk about it when the females in his family were not around. He told me and Pa about black men who'd been heroes in the war, like the soldiers in the 54th who had taken on Fort Wagner just a couple of years before. Mostly it seemed that Mose told us about black men dying. The year before, in 1864, General Nathan Bedford Forrest had captured Fort Pillow on the Mississippi River. Word was he butchered some whites and more blacks—even after some of them had raised the white flag in surrender. Another all-black regiment was wiped out at Poison Springs, Arkansas.

"James wrote a few letters early on," Mose said. "Told me about some Confederates who bring a black flag into battle."

Pa was as puzzled as I was. "A black flag? What for?"

"It's a sign," Mose answered. "Means they ain't gon' take no black prisoners."

"Mose," Pa began, "I can't help asking you if—"

"If I ever think about James dying? About him not coming back?"

Pa just nodded.

Mose chewed on the stem of his pipe. " 'Course I do. More often than I've a mind to. 'Specially since his letters stopped coming."

He turned and looked at Pa. "He won't be the first son I've lost. But if James goes, he goes fightin'. He'll have known what it's like to stand on his own and give and take like a man. Seems to me that's a knowledge worth dyin' for."

Every night my father would stagger back to the Bolton place, worn out from work. Sometimes he fell asleep before so much as raising a gourd to his lips. Fannie wouldn't stand for that, though. She'd wake him and make sure he ate something. "Oh, you can just give my share to Ezra," he'd say. Fannie would frown and say, "Don't you worry about Ezra, hear? A man's gotta eat if he's gonna work."

Other times Pa was right sprightly and would sit up and talk to Mose for hours, mostly about Mama and how wonderful she was. Some evenings, tired of listening, I'd stretch out on the ground and stare up at the stars. I'd hear Pa and Mose laughing inside or Fannie, Ruth, and Cinda singing while they swept or sewed. Paul usually went to bed early and slept as soundly as a log. "He's in his growing season," Fannie would say.

Once I was stretched out and watching the winking stars of the Drinking Gourd when Cinda came out and sat near me. She wrapped her arms around her knees and looked straight ahead into the darkness. I'd seen lots of girls during my short time in the world, but never had I seen one like her. Even in the pale starlight her pigtails gleamed like shiny ribbons.

I propped myself up on one elbow and looked at her.

She didn't say anything, and she didn't seem to notice, so I relaxed and let my eyes take her in. Finally I asked her what she was looking at. "The dark," she said.

"What's out there?"

"My daddy," she said. "He's out there in the dark. It makes me sad to hear his name sometimes, so I come outside and look way into the darkness. I want to be ready, see, because one day he's gon' come walking right out of it. Right out of the dark, just as sure as I'm sitting here."

"I know what you mean," I said.

Cinda shook her lovely head. "No, you don't."

"Do too," I said. "My mama's got to come out of that same darkness. I've been preparing myself for that. I prepare myself for the other thing too, in case she don't come at all."

"That's how you and me is different," Cinda snapped. She whipped her head around fast and stared at me, her eyes flashing. "I know my daddy's coming home. Ain't gon' be no other thing."

"I didn't meant to upset you," I said.

"Just shut up, then."

We both were quiet for a long time. Finally, she called my name. I didn't answer right away because I wanted to hear her say it again.

"Ezra?"

"Hmm?"

"Do you remember your mama at all?"

"Sometimes I think I do. I think I can remember her smile or her laugh or the way she scratched the side of her nose. But then I reckon those are things Pa told me about her. I was so small when she left."

"Not me," Cinda said. "I was nearly as big as I am now when my Daddy first ran off to fight. So I got plenty memories. . . . Ezra?"

"Hmm?"

"I'm sorry I sassed you before."

"Cinda, you can sass me anytime—I mean, if it will help you feel better."

Cinda smiled. "I do feel a little better."

"Well, then," I said. "Then it was worth it, wasn't it?"

"What do you do to feel better, Ezra?"

"Oh, I don't know. I think about when I was real young, and I try to remember what my father told me. He says my mama used to rock me close to her and sing me to sleep. Pa says I would snuggle close to her and look up at her face while she sang. She'd sing the sweetest lullaby."

Before I realized, I had begun to sing, not much louder than a whisper. Cinda took up the song, her sweet, sure voice joining my scratchy, less steady one:

> *De moonlight, a shinin' star,*
> *De big owl hootin' in de tree;*
> *O, bye, my baby, ain't you gwineter sleep,*
> *A-rockin' on my knee?*
>
> *Bye, my honey baby,*
> *A-rockin' on my knee,*
> *Baby done gone to sleep,*
> *Owl hush hootin' in de tree.*
>
> *He gone to sleep, honey baby sleep,*
> *A-rockin' on my, a rockin' on my knee.*

When we finished the song, Cinda leaned over and kissed me gently on the forehead. Her lips were so swift and light that they barely brushed my skin. "Good night, Ezra," she said. I was so stunned that I couldn't say anything.

Finally I managed to croak out a "good night." But it was too late. She'd already gone inside.

After we'd been on Roanoke for two weeks, Pa and some of the other men went to camp headquarters to see about wages. Pa hoped to get the building supplies we'd been promised or rations at the least. But there was no pay at all and no rations either. Superintendent James had refused to see the group. His assistant, Holland Streeter, quickly shooed them away. He told the men they should be grateful to be under the protection of the Union Army, that otherwise they'd still be in chains and planting cotton.

The men, some 30 in all, gathered outside Mose Bolton's place. "We're bein' worked like dogs fuh no pay and no food," one man said.

"I thought my massa was a devilish man," said another. "James and Streeter got enough evil between 'em to put ol' Satan to shame."

"They know we got to eat, or else we can't work," Pa said. "What could be takin' our rations so long?"

"Streeter and James is selling our rations," said Hiram Larkin. The group got silent right away.

"How you know that?" Jasper wanted to know.

Hiram flashed his rascally grin. "I drive a supply wagon. I go everywhere and I see everything."

"We oughta kill Streeter," someone shouted, "and James too!"

"Listen to yourself," Mose said with disgust. "We're badly outnumbered. They'd kill us for sho'."

"They killin' us anyway," Jasper retorted. "Fightin's quicker than starvin'."

"Hold on, hold on," Mose shouted over the growing clamor. "There's something else we can do. We can write a letter to the Freedmen's Bureau."

That was the first time Pa and I heard of the Freedmen's Bureau. It was a brand-new federal agency created for folks who'd just been released from bondage— folks like us.

Mose, who could read, had seen something about the Bureau in the *Colored Carolinian*, a newspaper made just for black people. With help from the men, Mose wrote a letter to General Oliver O. Howard, commissioner of the Freedmen's Bureau, complaining of our treatment and asking for assistance. "All we wants is a chance, and we can get a living like white men," was the last thing the letter said.

The next day Pa rushed back to the cabin right after work. He wanted to see Mose's newspaper, and so did I. Mose spread it out on his table and pointed out various groups of black marks and told us what they meant. I was fascinated, and I envied Paul and Cinda, who could already make out many words. Pa and I were both surprised by the notion of a paper for "colored" folks, as the *Carolinian* called us—and made by colored folks!

Pa's surprise turned to pure wonderment when Mose began to read the following lines:

> Information Wanted of Caroline Turner, who was sold from Nashville, Nov. 1st 1862, by John Dove to Sample (a trader then in human beings), who carried her to Atlanta, Georgia, and she was last heard of in the sale pen of Rupert Winslow (human trader in that place), from which she was sold. Any information of her whereabouts will be thankfully received and rewarded by her husband. Sam Lewis, Charleston.

We were quiet for a minute, so quiet that the only sound was Mose's and my breathing. Pa hadn't taken in any air since Mose stopped reading. Finally, Pa broke the silence.

"Mose, you think that man's gonna find his wife?"

"I don't know," Mose said. "But I do know one thing for sho'. It can't hurt matters none to do what's he done. Are you thinking you might do the same?"

"That's exactly what I'm thinking!" Pa could hardly sit still.

"Then we're wasting time," Mose declared. "You tell me what you want to say, and I'll write it down. We can send it out with our letter to the Bureau."

Pa's excitement had grown even more by the following afternoon. I was in the Boltons' cabin looking at words in the newspaper while Cinda and Paul patiently pointed out each letter to me. Suddenly we heard several explosions,

45

and Ruth came running inside. Instead of wearing her usual stern expression, she was grinning from ear to ear. Fannie rushed in from behind the house.

"Children!" she called. "I hear shooting! Is everyone okay?"

"Oh, Fannie," Ruth cried. "The war is over. The rebs have surrendered. James can come home now!"

Fannie pressed her hands against her chest as if she was trying to keep her heart from escaping. For a minute she couldn't speak. Then she managed to say "Lawd. Lawd. Lawd." Then she jumped into Ruth's arms. The two women held each other and danced around the cabin, sobbing all the while. Outside, the soldiers were setting off firecrackers and shooting their guns into the air.

Although Pa and the other men stopped work early, the celebration was in full swing by the time they arrived. Shooting and shouting and singing went on into the night. Pa and I did our share, laughing and clapping and singing along while a man played the fiddle and Hiram Larkin played the bones. He slapped two polished bones against his thigh and stomped his feet in tune to their clickety-clacking. Hiram could even grin while singing, throwing back his head and letting the words roll out between his big shiny teeth:

> *Abe Lincoln freed the nigger*
> *With the gun and the trigger;*
> *And I ain't goin' to get whipped any more.*
> *I got my ticket,*
> *Leavin' the thicket,*
> *And I'm a-headin' for the Golden Shore!*

46

Chapter 4

Our joy turned to heartbreak just 12 days later when word reached camp that President Lincoln had been shot on April 14. The man who'd worked so hard to bring us freedom was dead by an assassin's hand. An actor named John Wilkes Booth had shot Lincoln at Ford's Theater while the president and his wife were watching a play.

"I believe Lincoln was sent by God to do His will. He did it, and now God has called him home," Fannie declared. She had a strong and abiding faith. When it came to talk about God, salvation, and tribulation, she usually knew what she was talking about. She believed that Lincoln had been sent to lead us out of the wilderness of slavery. His job was done, and new leaders—anointed by God—would now have to step forward and show us the way. Mose had said many of the same things at a prayer meeting held a few nights before, to help send our

liberator's soul to its final resting place. Fannie had said
nothing at the meeting. She tended to let Mose do most of
the talking when they had an audience. But anyone who
spent time with the couple soon realized that Mose's ideas
were just as much hers.

She served hot corncakes while sharing her thoughts,
but nobody seemed to have much of an appetite.
"Granddaughter, you'd best get some meat on your bones
so that your daddy can recognize you when he comes," she
said to Cinda. "He sees you, and he's likely to walk right
on by." Cinda had taken to standing in the doorway of the
cabin, looking down the road. Fannie was right: She had
gotten thinner.

Some coloreds had already packed up and left
Roanoke, and others were making preparations. There was
still plenty of work to be had, but many of the soldiers no
longer cared. They were anxious to get home to their
families and resume their own lives.

The Boltons seemed reluctant to go anywhere,
thinking that the first thing James would do was head to
Roanoke Island. Pa and I weren't sure what we were going
to do. Having the freedom to make our own decisions was
still a new experience for us. Pa found work with Mose,
who'd arranged to do some carpentry for a local
landowner. Paul and Cinda spent time helping me with
my letters. We used the two copies of the *Colored
Carolinian* that Mose had and a recruitment pamphlet
that urged colored men to sign up and fight. Cinda's pa
had made up his mind to join the army soon after reading

just such a pamphlet. As Paul and Cinda helped me to understand the meaning of the pamphlet's many words, it became easy to see why James had become so inspired.

"This is our Golden Moment," the pamphlet proclaimed. "The Government of the United States calls for every Able-Bodied Colored Man to enter the Army for the THREE YEARS' SERVICE, and join in fighting the Battles of Liberty and the Union. A New Era is open to us. For generations we have suffered under the Horrors of Slavery, Outrage, and Wrong; our Manhood has been denied, our Citizenship blotted out, our Souls seared and burned, our Spirits cowed and crushed, and the Hopes of the Future of our race involved in Doubts and Darkness. But now the whole aspect of our relations to the White Race is changed. Now, therefore, is our most Precious Moment. Let us Rush to Arms!"

We also read from some of the letters James had sent before he stopped writing. Paul would go over his dad's messages with me while Cinda listened, mouthing each word as Paul came to it. She had memorized every letter her father had sent.

"Our men have become known for their bravery," one letter proudly observed. "Although the fighting has been very bad of late. Shells seemed to land all around us. One would explode and clear a space of twenty feet, and our men would move quickly to close the gap. The shells came so fast and furious that we had to retreat, a maneuver that turned out to be easier said than done. I'll never know how I got out of that skirmish alive. I dearly hope to see you all again, but if I do not, remember that I have given my life to a good cause. If we had a hundred thousand more colored troops like the men in this regiment, we'd end this war quickly."

In the following two weeks I learned a lot from my new friends. I learned to make out all the letters of the alphabet and the sounds that most of them made. Sometimes combinations of letters confused me, like *C* and *H* coming together to make the sound that begins *cherry* and *chair*. Paul and Cinda also taught me to recognize such words as *freedom* and *colored* and *Union*. During slavery it was very dangerous for slaves to learn to read, and those who did often pretended that they could not. We expected things to change now that slavery was over. Still, Mose cautioned us to never show too much learning in the presence of whites because there was no way to tell how they would react.

"Some are likely to respect you for it," he said. "But others might be just as likely to kill you. I've seen it happen. Once, about ten years ago I—"

"Oh, hush, Mose," Fannie interrupted. "Leave all that behind for once. You always thinkin' on the bad times."

"I'm just trying to teach these children a valuable lesson," Mose protested.

"They've got time ahead of them to learn all that," his wife replied. "We've all known freedom for just a little while. Let the children take some time and get used to it."

Mose looked as if he had something else to say, but he kept it to himself. I understood his intentions, and I appreciated what he was trying to do. All the same, I understood Fannie too. Looking back, I think that both of them were right. There were plenty of lessons we could take from slavery to help us cope with our freedom.

Mose and Fannie were two of the smartest colored people I'd ever seen. I'd known people like Luke and Pa, who seemed able to do anything except read. Mose was as good with his hands as Pa was, but he had plenty of another kind of knowledge too. Like her husband, Fannie had many valuable skills, and like him, she had a lot of bright ideas and a fine way of using words. I knew I'd miss the whole Bolton family when we parted, which turned out to be sooner than I expected.

Mose and Pa had spent many nights talking about Charleston, South Carolina, and the promising things happening there. A small population of colored men who'd already been free were welcoming their newly emancipated brethren. One of them was Thaddeus Cain, editor and publisher of the *Colored Carolinian*. He wrote forceful editorials urging his fellow blacks to come to Charleston. Once there, he argued, they could work together to make the city a place where blacks could better themselves without fear of punishment by angry whites, and by doing so set an example that the whole country could follow. Mose himself was inclined to join Cain and the others in Charleston, but he thought he should stay put, at least until he heard from James. He encouraged my Pa to go.

"Silas, you really ought to head out and see things for yourself," he told Pa late one night when they were poring over the pages of Cain's newspaper. Pa was especially fond of reading the advertisements seeking lost relatives. He hoped that his own bulletin would run soon and that somehow my Ma would find out about it. Mose seemed to know exactly what Pa was thinking. "Besides, if your Journee were to find your ad, she might head to Charleston or thereabouts."

Charleston had been where it all started, when Confederates attacked Fort Sumter and set off the war. Yet already there were colored men there who could think and speak for themselves and make a prosperous living besides. According to Mose, Cain believed that freed slaves needed to buy land as soon as possible. Pa wasn't so sure he agreed.

"Farming's brought us nothing but misery," he told Mose. "We've left a lot of blood in the soil. Maybe it's time we get our minds set on some other trade."

"I know what you mean," Mose said. "But still, Cain's words are worth a listen. The good Lord's not making any more land—least as far as we know. Might be wise to try to get your hands on some and hold on to it for awhile."

"Maybe," Pa said. "I got my doubts just the same."

That night as we lay in the Boltons' back room, Pa shared his fears with me. "I truly respect men like Mose and Thaddeus Cain," he began. "I'm sure they know more than I do, and there's plenty of wisdom in what they have to say. But white folks have always taken everything from us. Not just things, but the people we love too. Let's say we get ourselves a piece of that land. What's going to stop white folks from deciding they'd rather have it for themselves?"

"You're right, Pa," I said. "But not all white folks take from us. And sometimes when they do, they give it back. Remember that soldier, Pa? He gave back Mama's dress."

I couldn't see Pa, but I knew he was rubbing his chin in the dark. He always did that when he was thinking on a notion.

"He sure did," Pa said. "Hmmm."

He was quiet for awhile. Then he said, "I reckon we can't stay with the Boltons forever. Sooner or later we're bound to wear out their kindness. Besides, what Mose said about Journee might be true."

"So we're going to Charleston?"

"Yeah, I reckon so," Pa replied. "I got a little change from working with Mose, and he's been good enough to offer me a loan. Maybe we should move on while we have the chance."

Pa and I didn't have much more than the knapsacks we were carrying when we had first arrived. Fannie loaded us down with cornbread, biscuits, and chicken. She squeezed me real tight and looked at me with watery eyes. "You take good care of your daddy, you hear?"

"Yes'm," I replied. I was afraid that if I looked at her for very long I'd get teary too. Paul and Mose both gave us

53

hearty handshakes, and even Ruth managed to send us off with a smile.

Saying good-bye to Cinda was hardest of all. She was right thin because she'd had no appetite of late, and the dark circles around her eyes made it clear that she wasn't sleeping either. I felt I should say something really important to her, something that might soothe her hurt and offer her comfort to last all her days. But I was just a simple boy, and although I could now spell my own name, I didn't have the words to suit such a noble purpose. Sighing, I decided instead to just tell her the truth.

"Cinda, remember the night we stared into the darkness together? When the sky was heavy and low and full of stars? When you sang that song with me, the one my mama used to sing, you made me feel for a minute that everything was all right. It was like I'd forgotten all the bad things and knew nothing but good things. I didn't have any worries or cares."

"You were feeling free, Ezra," Cinda said solemnly. "I felt it too."

"Thank you for that," I said. "And for teaching me my letters. And for being my friend."

"Thank you," she said.

"Me?"

She smiled, her full lips folding back to reveal her large, shiny teeth. "Yes. For believing me when I say he's coming back."

It was my turn to smile. "When he gets here, will you tell him I was kind to his baby girl?"

"I'll tell him," she grinned. She hugged me, and for a minute I felt the same way I did when we sang together under the stars.

We were going to Charleston with Jasper Jones and Hiram Larkin. Hiram had talked his Union bosses into letting him have a wagon and two mules. He'd convinced them that the mules were old and half-blind, but in reality they were young and frisky. The corners of Jasper's mouth were still turned down, and he still grunted and snorted more than he actually said anything. Once you got used to him, though, he seemed to be a pretty good fellow. And I felt very protected in his company, the way I did with Pa. I believed that if any danger approached, Jasper would find a way to take care of it without blinking an eye or taking a step backward.

I thought a lot about Cinda when we first set out. At 10 I was much too young to think seriously about courting anyone, but I knew that when the time came I'd want someone like Cinda. Beautiful and wise and serious. I wondered if my mom possessed those same qualities. When Pa talked about her, he lingered over the same details. It was hard for me to get a sense of the whole person. If she was anything like Cinda, I figured, losing her must have been doubly hard. I didn't see why anyone would want to go a'courtin' in slavery times. What was the use of finding someone to love if that someone could be made to disappear at any moment? Still, it seemed that everyone did, in spite of the odds: Mose, Pa, Luke, Ruth. I bet even a crusty character like Jasper had a soft spot in his heart for some woman.

As for Hiram, I don't think he could stop talking long enough to land himself a sweetheart. He talked all the way from Roanoke to Charleston. We tried to stretch our victuals as long as we could. Jasper made snares and caught us some possum and swamp rabbits. At night we made a fire and ate. I should say that Pa, Jasper, and I ate. Hiram talked. He had a story for every day he'd spent in slavery—and I suspect half of them were made up.

"Say, Reverend," he says to Pa. "I call you that 'cause I seen you prayin' over your food. I fancy you a religious man."

"I am and I ain't ashamed of it," Pa said.

Hiram turned to Jasper. "What about you, Brother?"

Jasper grunted and sucked rabbit grease from his fingers. "I've had my fill of prayin'," he replied.

"My uncle Toby was a reverend," Hiram said. "He b'longed to Massa Jim Smith. Reckon y'all heard of him. Naw? I'll be. I thought everybody'd heard of him. He liked to work his slaves mornin', noon, and night. Sometimes they tried to run away."

At this Jasper stopped chewing on the chunk of rabbit he was holding and paid close attention.

"They had dogs to trail 'em with," Hiram continued. "So they always catched 'em, and then the whipping boss beat 'em most to death. Toby said it was awful to hear 'em hollering and begging for mercy. If they hollered, 'Lord, have mercy!' Massa Jim didn't hear 'em, but if they cried, 'Massa Jim, have mercy!' then he made 'em stop the beating. He say, 'The Lord rule Heaven, but Jim Smith rule the earth.'"

"That's quite a tale," Pa said.

Hiram beamed. "Thank ya, kindly," he said. Then he turned to Jasper to await his response.

For a long minute Jasper said nothing. He just stared at his chunk of rabbit. Finally he offered it to Hiram. "If I give you this, will you shut your mouth for the rest of the night?"

Hiram reached for the meat but Jasper pulled it back. "Not . . . one . . . word," he cautioned.

Hiram smiled, took the rabbit, and began munching happily. Jasper laid down, put his hat over his face, and quickly fell asleep.

The following afternoon we came across a body hung right over the road. He was a black man, and it looked like he'd suffered a lot before being strung up from the tree. He was naked to the waist, and dried streaks of blood formed dark stripes up and down the length of him. A message was painted on a piece of cloth and tacked to the tree trunk. Pa looked at me, but I shook my head. I couldn't make out the meaning of the words.

"We should say a prayer for this man," Pa said.

"You do that," said Jasper. "And while you're doing that I'll cut him down. He should be buried."

"Shh," Hiram said. "Anybody else hear that?"

We all sat quiet for a minute. I heard a light breeze rustling through the trees, and far away a crow hollered to its mate. A chill inched its way up my backbone. I felt like a doomed character in one of Paul Bolton's hant stories. Suddenly we all heard what Hiram had heard: someone whispering to us from a patch of tall grass near the road.

"Over there," I said softly.

"See, I told you I heard something," Hiram said a little too loudly.

A man emerged from the grass. We could see right away that his features were nearly the same as the dead man's. "That's my brother," he said. "His name is Bailey. Mine's Ben."

"Hey, Ben," Hiram said. "What did your brother do to get hisself done up so bad?"

Ben's eyes flashed. "Just be a man is all," he said. "I been watching him for four days, tryin' to keep the buzzards off."

"You got help now," Jasper said. "We can put him in the ground. You won't have to worry about buzzards no more." He produced a good-sized knife and commenced to studying the tree.

Ben stepped forward with one hand raised. "Obliged, friend," he said. "But we cain't, on account of that sign." He pointed to the words on the cloth.

"What does it say?" Pa asked.

Ben squinted at me and then looked back at Pa. "I'm sorry your boy had to see something like this," he said. "The sign say 'Anybody what takes down the body shall be hunged too.'"

Jasper snorted. "You think somebody's watching us right now?"

"Could be," Ben said. "We's takin' a chance for sho'."

After some discussion, we expressed our sorrow to Ben

and moved on. Jasper had wanted to stay and take a chance on burying poor Bailey, but Pa and Hiram wouldn't go along with his plan. For the rest of the day. Jasper's expression was more sour than usual.

Hiram had been spooked for a while, but by nightfall he was his usual talkative self.

"I knew an old slave woman name Sally who lost her mind," he said as we sat around our fire. Our supper was nuts and a broth made from rabbit bones. At the sound of Hiram's voice Jasper rolled his eyes, then leaned back and put his hat over his face. Hiram paid him no mind.

"She belonged to a man named Stingy Jack," he continued. "He sent her to get a bull tongue, which you know ain't nothin' but another name for a plow. But this woman, having lost her mind, ran down to the lot and tried to chase down a real bull. She set the barn afire and burned a dozen head of horses and three mules besides. Stingy Jack hung her sho' 'nuff. There was a big crowd to see it. The missus just cried and cried, on account she loved poor Sally and didn't know how she'd go on living without her. Missus told Jack he so mean even Satan ain't got no use for 'im. That the first person I ever seed hung. They used to hang folks a heap. The biggest crowds turned out to see it."

Jasper grunted and jumped up. He held his knife in his hand. The flames from the fire bounced off the blade, sending points of light in every direction. "That tears it," he declared. "Take my bags, and I'll join up with you in a whiles."

"Where you going?" Hiram asked.

"To put somebody in the ground," Jasper said. "And be glad it ain't you."

Pa spoke up. "Jasper, you're taking a big chance. I'm not sure it's worth it."

"Thanks for the advice, Silas," Jasper said evenly. "But I'm going all the same."

Jasper took off into the woods, heading back the way we'd come.

Hiram reached for the broth Jasper had left behind. "Some folks just don't 'preciate a good story," he said, taking a loud slurp.

We never saw Jasper again.

Chapter 5

Thaddeus Cain was a tall man, and nearly as wide as he was tall. He was hardly fat, though. You could see the muscles moving easily under his skin when he did something as simple as walk or talk or clap his hands in laughter. His fingers were thick, and his hands seemed as if they'd been carved from oak stumps. He had a voice to match. It sounded like low thunder rumbling in the hills. Although he had a sense of humor and enjoyed a joke as much as anyone, he could get serious before you'd notice the change in him, and he didn't suffer fools gladly. Before Pa and I ever laid eyes on Cain, we'd already gotten the idea that much of black Charleston revolved around him.

We pulled into town on a warm, breezy afternoon. The sun was high in the sky, beaming its golden rays on the busy residents of Charleston. Relying on the directions of kind strangers, we made our way to a general store owned and operated by a colored man and his three daughters. Hiram hitched our wagon right behind a wagon connected to a tall, dapple-gray horse with shiny red ribbons tied up in its mane. Inside the store, Oliver Walker welcomed us to his establishment. He was a thin, soft-spoken man with a warm smile. I took a look around while Pa introduced us. The place was small but very neat. One of Mr. Walker's daughters was sweeping. (Over time it occurred to me that someone was sweeping every time I entered O. Walker's Dry Goods Emporium. There never seemed to be a stray speck of anything on the floor.) Bins of flour, rice, sugar, and salt stood in rows. Bolts of cloth hung from wooden dowels. Canisters of tea, coffee, spices, and other foodstuffs lined the shelves. Molasses candy filled several jars on the front counter. At the back counter, a pretty lady in a fancy hat talked quietly with another of Mr. Walker's daughters. Mr. Walker asked about our journey.

"No problems along the way, I take it?"

"Well," Hiram began, "except for that hang—"

"We got along right easy," Pa interrupted.

"God often smiles on travelers," Oliver said.

"Except for black folk who ain't got they passes," Hiram said with a cackle. "Why, I remember this fool named Cato—"

Pa shot a stern look at Hiram.

"I tell you some other time," Hiram said.

"We're looking for work, Mr. Walker," Pa said.

"You're in the right place," Mr. Walker said. "There's

plenty of work to be had. There's a mine right outside of town, but that's not the first place I'd look. They can always use men on the docks. You oughta see Mr. Thaddeus Cain about that. He lives in a big house on Bull Street; it's not hard to find. And of course they need men in the fields. Mr. Cain can tell you where to look first. I'm not just talking about working for white men, mind you. Myself, I was born free, and there's others like me. I mean black men with land of their own and businesses to run. Uh, good afternoon, Miss Wells."

We all turned to take notice of the lady in the fancy hat. She was quite beautiful, coffee-brown with a long, graceful neck. She held her head high and seemed to float rather than walk. "Afternoon, Mr. Walker," she said, staring evenly at the storekeeper. She glanced quickly at us. "Gentlemen."

The faint scent of flowers hung in the air after she passed by. My father tried to tip his hat, but he'd forgotten that he was holding it in his hands. Hiram just grinned and said, "Well, I'm surely pleased to make your acquaintance."

But the lady was already gone.

Hiram whistled. "I wouldn't mind parking my shoes under her table," he said, still grinning.

"That won't happen, my friend," Oliver said confidently. "Miss Charlotte Wells is spoken for."

About two minutes later we heard a scream, followed by a horse's furious whinny. We rushed outside to find the dapple-gray rearing on its hind legs. The horse's forelegs scissored the air while it snorted and curled its lips behind its huge yellowed teeth. The red ribbons in its mane shook. In the wagon, the frightened Miss Wells tugged frantically at the reins. The horse planted its front hooves and swung around. The wagon's back wheels slammed against the hitching post, and the impact sent Miss Wells sliding from one side of the wagon seat to the other. The reins wrapped dangerously around her delicate wrist. In a flash Pa grabbed the dapple-gray by its bridle. Stretching his muscular arm, he stroked the horse's neck with his other hand, cooing in its ear until it stopped its fussing. When it was clear that the danger was past, Hiram stepped up and unwound the reins from Miss Wells's wrist. He reached up to help her down.

"Don't you worry, miss," he said. "You're in good hands now."

"Thank you kindly, sir," she said steadily. "But I really must be going." If you had walked up just then you'd never have known that she'd been screaming wildly just two minutes before.

Oliver Walker spoke up. "Won't you reconsider, Miss Wells? It might be good for you and the horse to set for a spell. I'll have one of my daughters bring you a cool drink."

"That really won't be necessary, Mr. Walker. And I'm not very thirsty either." She turned to my father. "But I am most grateful for your kindness, sir. Such bravery is not easily forgotten."

"My pleasure, ma'am," Pa said sheepishly. "I think she

just got a little spooked. She'll likely be fine from here on out."

"I hope you're right," she said. She clucked to the horse, who calmly raised her head and trotted away. Miss Wells held her head up high as she rode into the distance, her fancy hat sitting as neatly as a crown atop her hair.

"That's some fine lady," Hiram said as we all stared after her.

"And a proud one, too," Pa said.

"She's about as proud as you are lucky," Mr. Walker said.

"Lucky? How?" Pa looked curiously at the storekeeper.

Mr. Walker smiled. "Remember I told you that she was spoken for? She's the intended of none other than Thaddeus Cain. Once she tells him what you did, he'll be sure to help you."

"Long as he's not the jealous kind," Hiram said.

As we would come to learn, jealousy was beneath Thaddeus Cain. He was so sure of himself and so dignified that no one could imagine him actually worrying about what another man might do. But the day we went to his house to meet him, he seemed busy and distracted.

Cain's house on Bull Street was a good size, and while it wasn't particularly gaudy, it did have two tall columns supporting the front porch roof. Two sheds—each of them alone bigger than any slave cabin I'd ever seen—were on the property.

Cain sat in a twig rocker on his front porch. There

were three others before us, and we had to wait our turn.
We got in line. Hiram whistled. When he spoke, his voice
was hushed and filled with wonder, as if he'd seen an
angel—or a ghost. "I'd heard of folks like us that got their
own land and buildings and such like this, but I'd never
thought I'd see it with my own eyes." Hiram looked up at
Cain, trying to catch his eye. Cain seemed to see him but
didn't nod or anything. He kept right on listening to the
man and woman on his top step. When they stopped
speaking, Cain thought for a while, staring off into the
skies stretched out above his land. Finally, he told them
something we couldn't hear. They nodded energetically,
then half-bowed before they turned and began to walk
toward us. When they passed, I saw that both of them
were smiling.

Now there was just one man ahead of us. I'd seen some
dirty, raggedy clothes in my young life, but this man's
clothes were the worst I'd seen. They were filthy, and they
hung from this body in tattered strips. His boots, oddly
enough, were in pretty good shape. The dirt and filth he
had acquired had not yet managed to ruin the shine.

As the man approached, Cain frowned. "Sam," he said.
"Back already?"

"Afraid so, suh," said the man called Sam.

Cain leaned forward in his chair. The man had to
smell bad, but Cain gave no hint that he noticed. "What is
it this time, Sam? Surely you haven't come to settle your
debt."

"Very soon, suh. Very soon, I'll come and pay you
what I owe you."

66

"I don't mean to be rude, Sam, but why are you here?"

By now Sam was hopping around like a little kid struggling to hold his water. "A little something to tide me over," Sam muttered. He seemed to be looking past Cain at a mark just past his shoulder. Anything to avoid looking in his eyes, I guess.

"A little something, Sam? You've managed to lose every job this good community has provided for you. Not only do I not have any money to lend you, I don't have any place to refer you for work. No one will have you anywhere. You are all out of opportunities."

Sam looked down sheepishly, like a small child whose father has just scolded him for misbehaving. "Where can I go then?" he asked. His voice was soft and pitiful.

Cain was stern. "I suggest the Missionary Society," he said.

Sam turned to go, but stopped and turned around when Cain called after him. "Don't come back," Cain said. The raggedy man shuffled off, muttering to himself.

Finally it was our turn.

"Some people think I run a banking operation," Cain said. "They think I can print money in my basement, squeeze gold out of rocks, turn water into wine. I have no such illusions. I know my limitations." After a brief pause he spoke again. "Gentlemen," he said, "I'm Thaddeus Cain," though he had to know that we already knew who he was. Pa told him our names and that we'd come from Roanoke Island looking for work. Perhaps Cain was tired or discouraged by his strange conversation with Sam.

Whatever the reason, he didn't take to us right away.

"Why'd you pull up stakes and come here? Why not fight where you were?"

Hiram spoke before my father could open his mouth. "Not many women there, sir, if you catch my meaning. A man just starting out like I am needs a woman to help him with things. Some of us ain't much good by ourselves."

This seemed to move Cain a little. "Indeed," he said. "And you, Mr. Taplin, why did you come?"

"It was Mose Bolton's idea. He's my friend. He took me and Ezra in when we were on Roanoke. He told me colored men were organizing here, that it might be a good place to start again. Then, after he helped me place an ad in your paper . . ."

Cain interrupted. "You're looking for your people, right?"

Pa smiled. "Yessuh, my wife. Do you have any news of her?"

Cain raised one large hand. "Easy, man. I don't know if I have any news about her because I don't know who she is. A lot of people place ads, Mr. Taplin."

Before Pa could say anything else, Miss Wells drove up in her wagon. Cain rose from his chair. "I'm sorry, gentlemen. There's nothing I can do for you today, as my guest has just arrived. Once you've found lodging in the city, come by Zion Presbyterian Church. The Union League meets there, and you may be able to make valuable connections. Good day."

"But—" my father protested.

"Good day," Cain repeated, this time with an edge in his voice that told us he was not interested in continuing the conversation.

Sad, tired, and feeling a little hopeless, we turned on our heels—and ran smack dab into Miss Wells.

"I'm awful sorry, miss," Pa said, bending to pick up the lady's dropped parcels.

She recognized Pa right away. "Oh, my," she said. "It's my savior."

Cain looked puzzled. "Your what?"

Miss Wells smiled at her beau. "Why, darling, just an hour or so ago this man saved my life."

"You did?" Cain asked turning to fix his level gaze on my dad.

"All I did was calm her horse," Pa said modestly.

"Oh, it was much more than that," said Miss Wells. "Ashy was frightened by something, dearest. She reared up on her hind legs and nearly tossed me from the wagon. This man bravely stepped in and soothed the horse simply by whispering in her ear. It was the most amazing demonstration."

Hiram opened his mouth to say something foolish, but Mr. Cain silenced him by raising his hand. He kept his dark, smoldering eyes on Pa. "Mr. Taplin, would you say that you have a way with animals?"

"I can make 'em mind, if that's what you mean."

"I'm telling you, Thaddeus, he saved my life," Miss Wells said.

Mr. Cain said nothing. He just stared at Pa and tugged

at his whiskers. "What did you do back on the plantation?"

"Some of everything, suh. I was the foreman. I worked in the fields, I built cabins, repaired plows, whatever needed doing."

"Massa almost lost his mind when his son died fighting against the Union. Pa was just about running the place." I believe a full minute passed before I recognized my own voice. I hadn't meant to speak until I was spoken to, but I blurted those words before I could help myself. Everyone looked at me.

"You're awful proud of your papa, aren't you young fellow?" Cain was actually smiling at me now.

"Yassuh," I said.

"Then he must be taking good care of you. I respect a man who knows to look after his own." He looked again at Pa. "I've got sixty acres. I own them free and clear. I could use a man to supervise things, look after the livestock, make sure things are running smoothly."

"My Thaddeus is a busy man in town," Miss Wells said. She was suddenly a lot friendlier than when we first met her.

"We're all busy here, Mr. Taplin," Mr. Cain said. "None of us can afford to be idle. But sweet Charlotte is right. I'm a deacon at the church, an officer in the Union League and, of course, I've got my newspaper too."

"Thaddeus is just about the only colored man the whites will talk to," Miss Wells added.

"I was born free," Mr. Cain explained. "Many times

that wasn't much different from being a slave. It's true, though, that I had certain advantages, and I'm indeed grateful." He reached down and clapped me on my shoulder. "But now we're all free, and we're working with the Republicans to make sure that we stay free. What do you say, Mr. Taplin? Are you willing to work with me?"

Pa smiled. "Yes, suh, right away. If I could trouble you to lend me some tools I can get started on a cabin for me and my boy."

Cain laughed. It was the first time I heard his great loud laughter, and it would soon become one of my favorite sounds. "That won't be necessary," he said. "I've got cabins aplenty."

Pa smiled, then quickly grew serious. "My friend Hiram here is a good worker too."

Mr. Cain looked at Hiram. Hiram seemed to be a little afraid of Mr. Cain. He shifted from one foot to the other. "What can you do, Mr. Larkin?"

Hiram brightened. "Drive, suh. I've driven all over for the Union Army, and I've never met a wagon or cart I didn't like."

Mr. Cain looked at Pa. "It's true," Pa said. "Hiram drove us here."

Hiram looked hopeful while Mr. Cain tugged on his whiskers.

Miss Wells spoke up. "Thaddeus Cain, are you getting a notion?"

"Maybe I am, dear," he replied.

"I'll have you know that I'm perfectly capable of

driving myself anywhere I want to go," she huffed, folding her arms in front of her.

"Now, sweetheart," Mr. Cain said gently. "Just think of how much more you could get done with your new school if you could just set your mind on the important things, while someone else takes care of the little things."

"Like driving?"

"Exactly."

Miss Wells thought for a minute. Hiram looked so excited I thought he would burst open like a melon.

"It might make life a little easier for Ashy too," Mr. Cain prodded.

"Very well," she decided. "But I'll agree to this experiment for only a short while. Consider it a trial run and nothing else."

Mr. Cain turned to Hiram. "Is that acceptable to you, Mr. Larkin?"

"Yes, suh!" Hiram nearly shouted. "I'll take the lady anywhere she wants to go for just as long as she lets me."

"Then it's settled," Mr. Cain declared. He shook hands with Pa and Hiram.

"We're much obliged, Mr. Cain," Pa said.

"So am I," Mr. Cain said. "There's just one condition."

"What's that suh?"

"Most folks call me Thaddeus. You should too."

Chapter 6

Settling down in Charleston was like landing in another country. Or more like a country you'd been to in your dreams. Walking around in it for the first time, you couldn't be sure if you were really awake. You knew the language sure enough, but somehow things were different. Much different. Just months before we hadn't even belonged to ourselves. We worked hard and we prayed hard, but in the back of our minds we always knew that the little lives we scratched out could be wiped away at the whim of our masters. A bad crop, a loss at poker, an imagined insult, and we could be sent down the river, traded for a prize pig or whipped until our hearts gave out. On the plantation, just knowing how fragile our lives were was like a weight in our chests that slowed us down, made us step and breathe with caution. In Charleston, colored people stepped lively.

A free black named Denmark Vesey had planned a slave revolt here in 1822, but his attempt was foiled when authorities got wind of his scheme. Afterward, Vesey and his allies were hanged, and the city's whites cracked down on their fellow black residents, who outnumbered them by more than three to one. A standing militia was maintained, free blacks were heavily taxed, and the Negro Seamen Act called for the arrest of any black sailors who dared to leave port and walk the streets. Still, when Union troops reclaimed Charleston in 1864, a black regiment, the 55th Massachusetts, was the first to enter the city. Three thousand celebrating blacks, including Denmark Vesey's son Robert, stood and watched when the U.S. flag was raised again over Fort Sumter on April 14, 1865, just a few weeks before we arrived. Maybe that's why our people moved through the streets as if they belonged.

Other than what Mose Bolton had told us, Pa and I didn't know much about the town's recent history. We just marveled at the ease with which colored people went about their business, and we felt slow and timid beside them. In time we started to feel a little bit comfortable ourselves, and by summer we had begun to fit in.

I turned 11, and I wasn't the only living thing growing taller. Thaddeus Cain's corn was high. Pa worked with two other men, covering Cain's 60 acres. We lived on the property in a big cabin. It had a dirt floor, and we slept on pallets as we always had. We decorated the place a bit with some wood carvings Pa bought off a vendor and some beautiful curtains sewed by Precious, the oldest of Oliver Walker's three daughters. She was quite a seamstress.

"Got to keep your place pretty, Silas," she said. "When your wife come back she'll feel right special to see how you done it up." Precious talked so much about my mother coming back that it didn't seem natural. I got the feeling that she was getting sweet on Pa and wanted to know exactly what her chances were.

"It's not my place, Precious," Pa said. "But you're right. I gotta make it nice for Journee. Don't want her coming around to no shameful-looking shack."

There was even enough room for a little table where we could take our meals. Mr. Cain had a cook who prepared food for all of us, though he often ate in town. Pa and I liked to eat in town too, at the Missionary Society, where a home-cooked meal and companionship could be had for a couple of coins—or less if you were down on your luck.

The Missionary Society had a school too, held in the church basement, which most of the newly emancipated children attended. Children of Charleston's better-off blacks, usually ones who had already been free before emancipation, attended another school, a private establishment owned and operated by Miss Charlotte Wells. In truth I belonged with the other poor children, but Thaddeus Cain's lady said she just couldn't live with herself if she failed to welcome the son of the man who saved her life.

I'd taken a fancy to Miss Charlotte, as we students were allowed to call her. I liked to sit up front, on the low wooden bench nearest her desk, and watch her closely as each well-formed word came out of her mouth. She had a clipped, exact way of talking, like the Yankees who sometimes came around. Educated at an academy for colored girls in Philadelphia, she'd managed to remove much of our Southern drawl from her speech. I wanted very much to please her, so I studied hard. Soon I became more than comfortable with the alphabet and my figures too. But what I loved most of all was reading aloud, proudly reciting as Miss Charlotte pointed to each word written on her slate in her graceful, flawless hand.

At night I'd go over what I'd learned with Pa, picking words out of the *Colored Carolinian* and pronouncing them syllable by syllable. Sometimes Pa got mighty excited listening to me read. "Listen to my boy," he'd say. "Sound just like the schoolteacher. You may just grow up and be a schoolteacher yourself."

"Come on, Pa," I'd say. "Only ladies can be teachers."

"I don't see why that's so. You don't have to be a lady to be a learner. You shouldn't have to be one to teach. All I'm saying is a boy what's smart as you shouldn't have to work in nobody's fields. I don't want you to be no farmer."

"What's wrong with farming?" I asked him. I figured he was thinking I couldn't be good at it because of my foot. "Mr. Cain is a farmer."

"He's a gentleman farmer. These days he's more gentleman than farmer. He's got men like me working his dirt, men who can't do anything else."

I felt as if Pa was talking lowly about himself, and I didn't like it one bit.

"You can do whatever you set your mind to, Pa. Everybody knows that."

Pa smoothed out the yellowing newspaper spread out on the table before him. "We shouldn't be talking about me, Ezra. We're talking about you. You don't belong in a hot field breaking your back and blistering your fingers to fill another man's pockets. God gave you a good mind. It's up to you to put it to good use. Now that we free, ain't nothing to stop you."

"There's lots of land around here for cheap, Pa."

"I ain't of a mind to take a chance on it. I'm thinking I'll save some money, hire myself out to carpentry work like I was doing with Mose. Maybe be my own boss man someday."

"But Pa," I said. "I was down at Mr. Walker's store, and I heard him say colored folk should get while the gettin's good."

Pa snorted. "Oliver Walker should know better. He goes to Union League meetings just like I do. A man from St. Helena Island told us the Yankees are giving the land back to the Confederates what they took it from. Throwin' hard-workin' colored off the land, deed or no deed. Givin' 'em a chance to do sharecroppin' like that's some great thing. Ezra, land is the one thing God ain't makin' no more of. White men know that as well as I do. Thaddeus Cain is a good man, one of the best I ever met. I'm grateful to him, and I think highly of him, but if white men decide they want his 60 acres back, there ain't a God-blessin' thing he can do about it."

I'm sure Mr. Cain had thought about that a lot. He made plans to start other businesses, and he sent a lot of his money to be kept by relatives in Philadelphia. And at night he read the law. "I plan to know the white man's laws better than he does," I heard him say more than once. And I believed him, too. He ran the Union League meetings, teaching my Pa and the other men about the Constitution and the Bill of Rights, and a new law the Republicans were working on, something called the Fourteenth Amendment. Cain said the amendment would guarantee citizenship for everybody, even colored people.

Pa was always skeptical. "I'll believe it when I see it," he'd grumble after the meeting. Then he'd collapse onto his pallet and commence to snoring.

Cain got his law books from a sympathetic white man who'd been an abolitionist and now worked hard to improve living conditions for colored Americans. Henry Allen had been an adviser to Abraham Lincoln before returning to Charleston to resume his law practice. And, like me, he walked with a limp. He'd been wounded in an accident while a student at West Point. No one would deny that Mr. Allen was a brave and honorable man. Still, he had plenty of enemies among his own people, and some of his family had fought for the Confederacy. They called him a traitor, a Yankee in disguise.

But he didn't seem to care, and he continued to count Thaddeus Cain and other black residents of Charleston among his closest friends. Cain took Allen seriously when Allen suggested the study of law. Cain borrowed law books from his trusted friend. The volumes were big, fat, and full of fancy words that I could sound out but could make no sense of. Words like *ipso facto* and *Magna Carta*.

I figured those books were hard to read because simply carrying them was more than a notion. I discovered how heavy they were when Cain asked me to go to Allen's office and bring a certain book back to him. I was happy to do anything for him out of gratitude for all he'd done for Pa and me, but also because I was hoping to find a way to impress him somehow. I didn't know the word for it at the time, but I felt that Cain underestimated me, that he thought less of me than he should. I had nothing to base this on because he was as tolerant of me as he was of any other child, but it was a feeling I had nonetheless. So I jumped at the chance to run an errand for him.

Mr. Allen was waiting on the veranda of his office, which was located in a big, fine house in "white" Charleston. He was dressed in white from head to toe, and a fine gold watch hung from his vest by a shiny gold chain. His cane rested against the side of the rocker in which he sat. He watched me as I walked up the road, dragging my foot behind me. He smiled and stood up when I reached the porch.

"Afternoon, suh," I said, mumbling to my shoes. Much to my surprise, Allen placed his hand under my chin and gently lifted it until we were face to face. He leaned in close.

"It's okay to look me in the eye," he said. "In fact, I'd be insulted if you didn't."

I was stunned into silence. I'd never heard such words coming from a white man.

"Yassuh," I said. "Mr. Cain sent me."

"Of course," he said, still smiling. "I have the book right here. Be careful because it's very heavy."

All I could do was nod.

He pointed to my foot, then to his. "Looks like we have something in common."

"Yassuh," I said, trying to stare into his twinkling blue eyes without blinking. It was hard not to look away or stare at the ground.

"I got mine when a cross-eyed cadet made a colossal blunder," he said, wiggling his foot. "You ask me, Turner was way too blind to be at West Point. I suspect his daddy dropped a few gold nuggets into somebody's palm. How about you?"

I couldn't believe it. This rich white man was standing here talking to me like I was somebody important. Like I was white! I was so astonished that I nearly forgot that he had asked me a question. "Oh, I was born this way, suh," I replied.

"I see," he said. "Well, it doesn't seem to slow you down any. What's your name?"

I told him.

"Pleased to make your acquaintance, Mr. Ezra Taplin," he said, sticking out his hand. At first I thought he wanted his book back, then I realized what he wanted. Cautiously, I reached out and put my hand in his. He grasped mine and shook it firmly. "You give my best regards to Thaddeus Cain, you hear?"

I nearly floated back to Cain's place. A white man shook my hand! I was still pondering this dramatic occasion when I arrived at Cain's home. He opened the door himself. "Thank you so much, young Ezra," he boomed. "You must let me give you something for your trouble."

"No trouble at all, suh," I said.

80

"Nonsense. Old Allen's place is a good distance away, and you made it in excellent time. Come, come." He motioned me to follow him. Cain's house was not heavily decorated, but there was wood everywhere, and all of it gleamed. He turned from the corridor and crossed a threshold. What I saw when I entered the room made me almost forget everything I'd seen and heard in my whole lifetime, even the remarkable encounter I'd just had with Henry Allen. The entire room was filled with books. I gasped, not believing my eyes. Built-in shelves lined the walls from floor to ceiling. Every shelf was nearly warped from the weight of the books lined atop it. Not all of them were fat law books either. The titles of some of them made me guess they were made-up stories—*A Tale of Two Cities, Moby-Dick, The Scarlet Letter, Uncle Tom's Cabin.* I craned my neck and tried to take them all in.

"Ezra," Cain thundered. "Do close your mouth before you swallow a swarm of flies."

"Yassuh," I mumbled, never taking my eyes off the shelves. My mouth stayed open.

"I take it you've never seen a library before?"

"Massa Stewart had some books," I said. "But nothing like this."

Cain chuckled and pulled a chair out from the immense oak table in the middle of the room. "Please sit down," he said.

I sat while he reached and pulled a slim volume from a shelf. He opened it and placed it in front of me. "See if you can make out any of the words."

I was surprised. I figured Miss Charlotte had told him

81

what a good reader I was, how I was the best student in her class, better even than Patience, Mr. Oliver Walker's youngest daughter. And she was 14 years old.

I turned to the book and studied the first line. I'm proud to say that I stumbled only on the first few words, then began to recite smoothly and with confidence, as if I'd read the words many times before. It was a magical experience: I felt the author's voice inside my head, guiding me as I spoke.

> I was born in Tuckahoe, near Hillsborough, and about twelve miles from Easton, in Talbot county, Maryland. I have no accurate knowledge of my age, never having seen any authentic record containing it. By far the larger part of the slaves know as little of their ages as horses know of theirs, and it is the wish of most masters within my knowledge to keep their slaves thus ignorant. I do not remember to have ever met a slave who could tell of his birthday. They seldom come nearer to it than planting-time, harvest-time, cherry-time, spring-time, or fall-time.

Now it was Thaddeus Cain's turn to gasp. "My dear boy," he said. "might you have seen this book before?"

"No, suh," I answered. "Miss Charlotte has been teaching me. She says I'm making commendable progress."

"Indeed. Indeed," he said, barely able to contain his excitement. "Do you know who wrote this book?"

Before I could reply he turned the book over and showed me the cover. It said, *Narrative of the Life of Frederick Douglass, An American Slave, Written by Himself.*

Then he turned to the first page and showed me the words written there in flowing script: "To Thaddeus, My Dear Friend and Ally. Yours in the Cause of Liberty, Frederick Douglass."

I didn't know then who Douglass was and why he was so important, but I was curious to know more. There was no time that day, however, as Cain pulled down book after book from his crowded shelves, challenging me to read a few lines from each. This I did successfully, and each time my host would gasp or chuckle. "My dear boy," he said again and again, "I believe you have discovered the power of the word."

Sleep was nearly impossible for me that night. I tossed and turned on my pallet, holding in my hands a present from Thaddeus Cain. It was a collection of stories by Washington Irving. I read it by candlelight until Pa ordered me to bed.

I clutched the book and thought about the events of the day, a day that proved to be a turning point in my life—a day I knew I'd remember forever. I'd met a white gentleman who insisted on treating me as an equal. Mr. Allen's warmhearted manner made me think of other whites I'd encountered who'd been different from the others. There was Missus, who fed us johnnycakes in the shadow of the Big House; Mr. Crowder, the Union sniper who'd stopped Sam Logan from hurting Pa; and even the fat private who'd given back my mother's dress. I knew there were plenty of whites right there in Charleston who hated me something powerful just because of the color of my skin. I knew that just the thought of people like me going about freely was enough to turn their stomachs. And I also knew that they were holding their own meetings at the same time Pa and the other colored men were having Union League gatherings. Pa told me angry whites were talking about taking up arms again, using guns to drive colored people off their land. But knowing all that didn't worry me. Just knowing about men like Mr. Allen gave me hope.

And I'd made another, even more important discovery. For the first time I fully understood the power of the word. Back on Roanoke, when Paul and Cinda showed me the recruitment notice that sent their father to war, I'd first seen how letters on a page could move men to tears or excitement or even to action. After my visit to Cain's library I became certain that I wanted to be a man who could use words in a way that touched other's men's hearts. I wanted to be a man like Thaddeus Cain.

I called across to my father in the darkness. "Pa," I said.

"Yeah, son."

"You don't have to worry about me being a farmer."

"No?"

"No. I'm going to be a writer."

Summer drifted into fall. Pa looked after the harvest, which promised to be bountiful. Mr. Cain let me borrow more books in exchange for keeping his library tidy. He even gave me an old ledger book, which he suggested I use "for jotting down important thoughts and pearls of wisdom."

One afternoon a letter for Pa arrived at Mr. Walker's

store. Hiram told Pa, and Pa nearly broke his neck hustling over there. I knew he was hoping for word from my Ma. His advertisement had run in the *Colored Carolinian* all summer long without attracting any response. But the letter turned out to be from Mose Bolton. Pa was a bit disappointed but still eager to hear from his friend. I read him the letter right outside the store.

> *Dear Silas,*
>
> *How are you, Brother? I hope that the Good Lord continues to shine his bountiful blessings upon you. Have you learned any news of your beloved wife? How is your boy? I bet he's a lot bigger. Our Paul is looking me straight in the eye. Mother is fine, and so are Ruth and Cinda. We have all been feeling much better since our James came home. He was wounded in the final days but with the Lord's blessing should live to see many more sunrises. He took a ball in the arm but lucky for us they did not need to remove his limb. The shot caught mostly the fleshy part of his arm. He and Ruth are expecting a blessed event again after all these years. But I can fill you in on these matters when I see you again. I'm writing to tell you that James and I plan to be in Charleston this fall for the Colored People's Convention. It will fill my heart with gladness to see you once again. These are important and promising times for us, my Friend.*
>
> *Yours in Jesus,*
> *Mose Bolton*

Chapter 7

Charleston was chilly by mid-October, and it wasn't just because of the crisp autumn air. Tension between the races was once again on the rise. The white men in town seemed angrier than usual. Their cheeks flamed bright red when they saw us approaching, and they often seemed eager to turn casual encounters into confrontations by bumping into us as we passed. More than once I was shoved to the ground while running errands for Mr. Cain. Hurtful phrases whites muttered in conversation rose above the noise of the streets, assaulting our ears: "Damned blacks." "Enough is enough." "Too big for their britches."

Change was afoot once again, and every colored person knew it. How we would respond became a constant concern.

Hiram Larkin noticed little of this, for he was in love. He'd met Malindy Johnson and fallen for her like a sack of rice. She was a cook in "white" Charleston, a pretty woman with a round brown face and bright eyes. Like Hiram, she was a loud talker who loved to laugh. They took to strolling around together in every spare moment, holding hands, giggling, cooing, and calling each other pet names like "Sweet Potato" and "Honey Man." We all figured that it wouldn't be long before wedding bells rang in Zion Presbyterian.

The two of them together were almost too much to take for dignified folks like Mr. Cain and Miss Charlotte, who were much quieter about their courting. It bothered Pa too, although Hiram didn't stick so close to him like he did when we first arrived. I think it hurt Pa to see any couple in love because it reminded him of what he was missing. Precious Walker used to perk up each time she saw my Pa enter the store, but even she found it hard to summon a smile after a while. He always came in looking for the same thing: a letter from my mother.

Pa worked hard as usual, throwing himself into his labors to keep his mind off his loneliness. I hoped that he found some comfort in my growing up. I'd learned enough about life by now to understand my father's situation, at least a little bit. I realized that my company couldn't fill all the empty spaces in his life, no matter how much he loved me. Sometimes in the evening we'd sit together in our cabin without talking, each of us alone with our thoughts. I'd find myself remembering Cinda, her pigtails, the look on her face as she stared up at the stars. I was happy that her father had come back—

wounded but alive. Now she wouldn't have to stand at her door and peer into the darkness anymore, and hopefully she was eating more and taking care of herself again.

She'd be proud of me, I was certain. She'd be impressed by my "commendable progress" in Miss Charlotte's class, my still-growing love of reading and writing. I resolved to write her a letter and give it to Mose Bolton when he came for the convention. I'd tell her about young Goodman Brown and Oliver Twist, characters I found on the shelves in Mr. Cain's library. I had a much bigger picture of the world now, and I wanted to show her somehow. Maybe I'd share some of my "pearls of wisdom" from my ledger diary.

Mr. Cain published a special issue of the *Colored Carolinian* for the convention delegates. Unlike the publishers of the "regular" papers in Charleston, he had no printing press of his own. He assembled his articles and ads at his home and sent the manuscripts to a sympathetic printer in Philadelphia. There the type was set and the finished papers smuggled into Charleston under cover of darkness. It was not illegal for blacks to publish newspapers, but the messages they expressed often aroused the anger of whites. Angry mobs had killed some colored journalists and destroyed their presses. Mr. Cain even told me about a white abolitionist, Elijah Lovejoy, who'd had three printing presses taken from him by proslavery mobs. When he tried to hold onto his fourth press, his hostile neighbors shot him to death.

Much of Mr. Cain's paper was made up of "seeking

family" ads like Pa's. It also contained church notes, notices of marriages, new businesses, and offers of trade. But editorials were the most important—and most dangerous—part of the paper. It was the section that whites read most carefully, but Mr. Cain didn't allow that to discourage him. He fearlessly pushed for full citizenship for America's colored citizens, informing his readers of various state governments' efforts to turn back time and return blacks to a state of slavery or something close to it. He also published letters from a man known only as Telemaque. Telemaque's letters—as well as pamphlets that turned up at various places—argued forcefully for blacks to aggressively defend themselves from white aggression, even if they had to take up arms and form militias. Telemaque's ideas enraged many whites. One ex-Confederate officer pledged 500 dollars to anyone who could locate and "detain" Telemaque. If Mr. Cain knew who Telemaque was, he wasn't telling.

I was honored when Mr. Cain asked me to help him with the issue. While we worked he told me about other publications like his, like the *North Star*— begun by Frederick Douglass himself—and *Freedom's Journal*, the very first colored paper. Mr. Cain printed the same quotation from *Freedom's Journal* in every issue of the *Colored Carolinian*: "From the press and the pulpit we have suffered much by being incorrectly represented. We wish to plead our own cause. Too long have others spoken for us. Too long has the public been deceived by misrepresentations, in things which concern us dearly."

In the special issue, Mr. Cain planned to tell his readers about the Black Codes being proposed around the country. In state houses throughout the South, lawmakers were passing laws that restricted the rights of colored people to live, work, and conduct business. The South Carolina Black Codes were especially harsh, according to Mr. Cain.

"These laws," he wrote, "make a mockery of the glorious concepts of life, liberty, and the pursuit of happiness, which our nation's illustrious founders held inseparable from their birthright as citizens of this fair Republic. Is this the freedom for which our brothers fought and died?"

The codes forced black laborers and craftsmen to buy costly licenses in order to practice their trades, barred blacks from sitting on juries or joining the state militia, allowed policemen to easily arrest blacks for being homeless, and placed invisible chains on black apprentices by forcing them to obey their masters. Cain urged the convention delegates to draft a resolution calling for the repeal of the codes. He ended his editorial with lyrics from a song that he said was a favorite of colored convention-goers everywhere:

> *Ours is not the tented field—*
> *We no earthly weapons wield*
> *Light and love our sword and shield,*
> *Truth our panoply.*

"Goodness, look at you," Mose Bolton said with a

smile. He was standing outside O. Walker's Dry Goods Emporium. "Growing like tobacco, I'd say." He shook my hand then rubbed my head. Mose seemed kind and wise as ever but somehow younger. There was an extra bounce in his step. He turned to Pa. "What're you feedin' this young'un?"

"Must be the free air," Pa said, grinning. "We all know free air does healthy things to a body."

"Do tell," Mose said. "I always tell Mother that slavery air stole a few inches from me. If it wasn't for that I'd be six feet high."

James Bolton was six feet and then some, tall as my Pa. He had the straight posture of a soldier and proud stride of a man who'd fought for his freedom. Even with his arm in a sling he looked powerful. When he smiled he looked a lot like Mose.

"This here's my son, James," Mose said.

"It's an honor to meet you," Pa said, shaking his hand. "I don't have much, but any son of Mose Bolton's welcome to anything I got."

"Much obliged," James replied. "I'm thankful to you for helping my family while I was away. I've heard nothing but good things."

"You have a beautiful family," Pa said. "God has smiled on you for sho'."

"So this is the great Ezra Taplin," James said, extending his hand.

"Sir?" (Miss Charlotte's crisp Yankee speech was beginning to affect my tongue.)

"My Lucinda goes on and on, talking about Ezra this and Ezra that. I think that girl's carrying a flame for you, and she just going on thirteen."

My face felt hot, and my heart fluttered a little in my chest. Cinda? Carrying a flame? For me? I felt dizzy.

"Take a breath, boy," I heard my Pa say. "Land sakes, I better get him a sip of water before he passes out."

The Boltons bunked with us. Mose and James joined Pa at our table after settling their belongings in a corner. I sat on the floor nearby.

"Might as well have chains on my ankles," Mose complained. "Can't do carpentry without a license. Can't get a license without money. Can't make money without doing carpentry. They trying to force us back into the fields. They doing that on the Sea Islands now. Soon they'll be doing it everywhere."

"They" were white folks.

"Forcing us back into their fields," James said. "They wait until you've paid for the deed, paid your taxes, and sunk all your money into your crops. Then they take it all back."

"Must be somethin' we can do," Pa said.

"Tell you what I'm going to do," James said. He had a faraway look in his eyes. "I'm going West."

Pa looked at him curiously. "West?"

"West," James repeated. "Kansas or someplace."

"Listen to the corporal," Mose said.

"There's more land out there than white folks know what to do with. Don't take much to buy a bunch of acres."

"It's more than a notion," Mose added.

Pa shook his head. "I don't want nothin' more to do with land. I can't see white folks ever gettin' enough of it. I fear for any colored man who gets in between a white man and a parcel of dirt."

"Then you're going to pay for a carpentry license?" Mose asked.

"I might, when I get more saved up," Pa replied. "I'd rather pay with money than with blood." He turned to James and nodded toward his shoulder. "I look at you, and I figure colored men have done enough bleedin' for a while."

The Walker family's general store was very busy while the convention delegates were in town. Oliver Walker was a delegate himself, and after sessions folk would gather around to talk about the day's proceedings. The fact that Precious and Prudence, his two oldest daughters, were marrying age helped keep the place popular too. Men kept suddenly running short on supplies and would have to return for one or two more items. According to Mr. Walker and Mose, most of the men and all of the leaders were free-born. Former slaves made up just a small number of the men on hand.

Saturday afternoon I was sitting under an oak near the store, chewing on a molasses candy. Soon, just as I figured, the men gathered around for a convention update. Pa was working on Mr. Cain's land, so I prepared to fill him in on the news of the day. I saw Hiram wiping his face with a damp kerchief. It was the first time I'd seen him without

Malindy in a long while.

"There's a new group in Tennessee," Mr. Walker announced to the assembly. "They call themselves the Ku Klux Klan. They wear hoods over their faces, and they ride at night, scaring colored off their land. Those that don't run get killed."

"Think they'll come here?" somebody asked.

"God forbid," said Mr. Walker.

"If they do, we should fight fire with fire," said another man.

"How we are going to do that? The new codes make it against the law for us to carry guns. Besides, that's what Denmark Vesey said and look at what it got him: a hanging on Ashley Avenue."

"It's the federal government's job to stop them," another voice shouted.

"I wouldn't be surprised if the Klan is the federal government," another hollered.

Another man demanded proof that the Klan was real and not a rumor.

"Talk to Jed Rivers," Mr. Walker said. "His own brother got killed by the Klan. Jed found him swinging from a tree."

"Lawd, Lawd, Lawd," somebody said. There was a brief silence while the information sunk in. Finally someone else spoke up.

"They been hangin' us a long time. Ain't like this Ku Kluck's startin' somethin' new."

I stood up to see who the voice belonged to. The speaker was a very old man. He was small, and his eyes were weak and watery. White stubble streaked his face, which was so black it was almost blue. I suspected he could see no more than a few feet in front of him. His voice was surprisingly strong.

"This is Ambus Hope," Mr. Walker said. "He came all the way from Arkansas just to attend the convention."

"I came from Arkansas, but I spent most of my life here in South Carolina," Mr. Hope said. "Y'all talkin' 'bout hangin'. They used to hang folks all the time. Big crowds turn out to see it. The men would hang us and set us on fire and the women and children would eat their supper while we burned. They called theyselves the Upper League then. Maybe they call theyselves the Ku Kluck now. Don't make no difference. They ride by night, and we die by day."

I don't remember much of what was said after Ambus Hope stopped speaking. I doubt anyone else did either because no one was in the mood for listening or talking anymore. Mose Bolton had already told Pa much of what had happened at the convention. Of course, he hadn't heard the old man talking about the Upper League. Lucky for him. That night I dreamed I was on the road to Charleston again, at the spot where we saw a dead man named Bailey hanging from a tree. Pa and Hiram and Jasper were nowhere in sight. I stood there beside Bailey's sad-eyed brother, and together we tried to keep the buzzards away. The more we flailed at them the faster they flew, attacking us in thick swarms like bees. We struggled in front of a large crowd of white women and children. They had blankets spread out on the grass and huge heaps of food piled all around. They munched happily and laughed at our feeble efforts.

The next day was a happy one for Mose Bolton. After Pa explained to Mr. Cain that Mose was responsible for our journey to Charleston, Mr. Cain graciously offered to take supper with Pa and the Boltons after the last session of the day. Both Mose and James were eager to find out what the publisher of the *Colored Carolinian* thought about opportunities in the West.

Outside Oliver Walker's store, all the talk was of Edisto Island. Just one month before, the government had sent Oliver Howard, head of the Freedmen's Bureau, to the Sea Islands to order the freedmen to abandon their claim to the land and return to work for the men who had owned them before emancipation. To make matters worse, President Andrew Johnson had thrown his support behind the Confederates—the very same men who'd fought to secede from the Union that Johnson now led. The freedmen of Edisto Island were enraged. They sent a petition to Johnson asking him to change his mind. So far he had given no sign that he would.

Mr. Walker read from the special issue of the *Colored Carolinian*, reminding his audience how the Black Codes affected our freedom to live and pursue honest work.

"I hear in Georgia they made it against the law for black folk to laugh." It was Hiram, shuckin' and grinnin' like always.

"Mr. Larkin," Oliver Walker said, "Laughter has its time and place."

"Well, in Georgia, colored people can't laugh outdoors.

They got to laugh in big barrels. That's what I hear anyway. They got these big barrels you got to stick your head in, and it's always a long line of folks waitin'. Sometimes they just give up and go home. That's why so many colored folk in Georgia got big heads. They all swollen from holdin' that laughter inside."

Several of the men started laughing. Even Mr. Walker, dignified as ever, snickered a time or two. "All right," he said. "All right. Thank you, Mr. Larkin, for breaking the tension. I'm afraid, though, that we won't be laughing if these codes are allowed to stand."

The discussion was back on track. "They won't stop until we're in chains again," someone shouted.

"That's why we have to work together," Mr. Walker said.

"Well, what's the convention going to do?" someone demanded.

"We're preparing a statement," was Mr. Walker's reply.

That night, Mr. Cain, Mr. Walker, and other leaders of the convention stayed up almost until dawn, writing and revising their petition. The next morning's session—the last—was spent getting the language just right. Three men, one of whom had once been a personal secretary to Frederick Douglass, were each assigned to write out a copy of the final draft.

It seemed like nearly all of the colored people in town were gathered outside Zion Presbyterian Church when the delegates exited for the last time. Word had traveled quickly that Thaddeus Cain would read the Proceedings of the Colored People's Convention of the State of South

Carolina to interested parties. Most of the adults were crowded near the front of the steps. I stood a little off to the side with Miss Charlotte, Patience Walker, and my other classmates.

"Good afternoon, fellow Carolinians," Mr. Cain thundered. You could easily hear his rich bass voice from where we stood. "I have here the final version of the petition drafted by the Colored People's Convention that assembled here over the past several days."

Mr. Cain spoke like a seasoned orator, searching the crowd and making eye contact as he talked. His eyes met mine, and I smiled—then frowned in confusion when he paused. He beckoned me, but I figured he was motioning to someone else. I pointed at my chest. He nodded.

"Ladies and Gentlemen, the proceedings will be read by my friend and valuable assistant, Ezra Taplin."

"Go on," Miss Charlotte urged. "Make me proud."

Astonished, I made my way to the front of the crowd. I was standing next to Mr. Cain sooner than I wished. "You want me," I whispered. "I can't—"

"Of course you can," Mr. Cain assured me. "It's only words."

I took a deep breath and tried to forget all those eyes on me. Mr. Cain was right. They were only words. And like the words in Frederick Douglass's autobiography, they came to me easily. "To the Honorable Senate and House of Representatives of the State of South Carolina," I began. "We, the colored people of the State of South Carolina do hereby appeal to you for *justice*."

Chapter 8

Dear Cinda,

Are you surprised to get this letter? As you can see, I've made "commendable progress" with my reading and writing. I will always be grateful to you for getting me started. It was good to see your grandfather again. He is as wise and kind as I remember. Your father is everything you said he was, brave and smart. I am glad to hear that all of the Boltons are doing well. Please say hello to everyone for me, especially Paul. I can still taste your grandma's cornbread and molasses, even after all this time.

Pa and I are doing fine. Pa works for Thaddeus Cain, an important colored man, whose name you might remember. He is editor and publisher of the <u>Colored Carolinian</u>. He owns 60 acres of good land, lends money to help freedmen buy property, and is a leader of the *colored people here. Have you ever seen a library? It's a room full of books, and Mr. Cain has one in his house. He even lets me borrow books from him. I do small jobs for him in return.*

Let me tell you about the most exciting day of my life—so far. When the Colored Convention was over, Mr. Cain let me read the proceedings to the crowd gathered around the church. At first I was afraid but soon I felt fine. Everybody clapped and cheered when I was done. I know they were really cheering the ideas that I read, but I like to think that some people were clapping for me, a little colored boy setting free the power of words.

Your father says you may be moving west. I don't know, Kansas seems so far away. Your grandfather was the one who told us about Charleston, so I figured your family would come here too. If you do go west, please don't forget me. I will never forget you.

Your friend,
Ezra Taplin

Chapter 9

Sometimes when something unforgettable happens, you can look back on it and recall that God or Nature had given you a sign. You might remember a wagon turning a corner and splashing you with mud, or a hoot owl calling your name. If you're paying attention, you can take note of such a thing and prepare yourself for what's to come. That's if you're lucky. If you're unlucky, you get no warning at all. That's how it was one day when I was bringing Mr. Cain a book from Mr. Allen's office. There wasn't a hint of breeze, not a low-lying cloud to be found. The hoot owls were all hidden, and the air was so balmy that you couldn't tell winter was approaching unless you had a calendar or an almanac.

I'd gotten so used to coming in and out of Mr. Cain's house that I often entered without knocking. I came in toting yet another heavy law book when I heard voices in the library. They belonged to Mr. Cain and Pa. My father hardly ever came to Mr. Cain's house, and when he did he seldom went past the veranda. It seemed to be a point of pride to him, as if he was somehow unwilling to approach his boss in such expensive surroundings. But there he was.

They hadn't heard me come in. I was still in the foyer when I heard Mr. Cain say, "Silas, I'm sure you know that I think the world of you and your boy. Thanks to you, I had a record harvest, and Ezra's skill with numbers and letters contributes to my paper's success. We get along well, and in a short time we have become close friends."

I could hear Pa's chair groan as he shifted in his seat. "We like you too, Thaddeus," he said, "but I can't believe you called me over here to tell me that."

Mr. Cain let out a low chuckle. "Like most hard-working men you get right to the point. I admire that. I've got no heirs, Silas. When I go, what little I have goes with me. Running a colored newspaper, fighting for freedmen's rights—it's all risky business. Get enough people angry, things can happen. I could go anytime."

"I've seen more people 'go' than I care to remember," Pa said. "I ain't much for thinkin' on death."

"You've got no choice. We didn't make this world, but we must live in it all the same. That means we have to be prepared to leave it, whether it's someday soon or at some distant future date. But I didn't call you here to tell you that either. I called you here to ask you to become my business partner. It's true that I haven't known you long, but I've had the opportunity to study you closely, and I've come to believe that God brought you here for a reason. I trust you, Silas. As my partner, you can continue to run the agricultural enterprises, while I can oversee the newspaper and work to incorporate my lending services. Colored folks have been treating me like a bank for years. It's time I became one. You'd be entitled to half the profits."

A long silence told me that my father was thinking on what to say next. Finally, he responded with a question. "How come you've got no heirs?"

I sat down quietly, carefully setting the large book on my lap.

"I never had the chance," Mr. Cain replied. "Had a wife, though, but she was a slave. I was born free, remember. My grandfather was a white man of wealth and power. He never openly acknowledged his paternity of my own father, but he secretly provided for him. He educated him at a free school in Philadelphia and helped him set up his own business here. I got my schooling in Philadelphia too, and I would have stayed there. When my father died, I returned to Charleston. I met Esther and fell in love. I called her my wife and she called me her husband, but we were never officially married. Her owner was a jealous man, a crazy man who drank too much. One day he killed her in a rage."

"My Lawd," Pa said softly. "I'm sorry."

"I'm sorry too," Mr. Cain said. "Still sorry after all these years. We never had time for children. Not that we didn't want them."

"What about Miss Charlotte?"

I heard the heavy tread of Mr. Cain's boots as he paced around the room. "I'm very fond of Charlotte, as she is of me. But I'm not sure if we should be married. I'm fifty-four years old, and she's much younger. We've agreed to give the subject further consideration. In the meantime, there is my work. I've made great progress in the study of the law with the help of my—I suppose I can tell you— my cousin, Henry Allen. My grandfather was also Henry's."

That made sense to me. Mr. Allen had the same fearless glint in his blue eyes that Mr. Cain had in his brown ones.

"You must have known Denmark Vesey," Pa said, "or your father must have. I seen the tree on Ashley Avenue, the one they hanged him from."

"Folks say that," Mr. Cain said. "But the truth is none of us really knows where he was killed. My father knew Vesey, and so did I. His house was on Bull Street too, not far from ours. He had a few mulatto lieutenants, but mostly he had no use for light-skinned blacks like my father. When they caught him, I was eleven, just like your boy. Word got out that a revolt was afoot. White folks were afraid to go to sleep because they thought the slaves were going to break loose and burn them in their beds. Some white families stood outside their houses all night, watching and waiting for the mobs of torch-bearing blacks. But it didn't happen, and Vesey and all his assistants were quickly tried and hanged. The *Charleston*

Courier had one sentence about the execution—one sentence. That's when I first got the idea of starting a colored newspaper. But I was just a boy, and my father sent me to Philadelphia soon after.

"Enough family history, Silas," Mr. Cain continued. "What do you think of my proposition?"

"I'm honored, Thaddeus, but you know how poor I am. I can barely earn my keep as it is. I know I can't buy half of your business."

"You're rich in spirit and character, Silas. You and Ezra both. It's for that reason that I'm not offering to sell you half of my business; I'm simply offering you half of my business. Say you'll join me, Silas. Say yes."

"We'd have to look into other things beside land," Pa said. He still had little faith in farming.

"I told you I'm already doing that. We're in agreement, Silas. And consider this: Someday Ezra could have his very own newspaper to run. It's a dangerous business, to be sure, but he's got a way about him that says he could handle it."

I wanted very much to rush into the room and urge Pa to say yes, but fear and anticipation held me to my spot on the floor.

"I'll do it," Pa said.

"Wonderful!" Mr. Cain proclaimed.

I heard the clink of glasses as Mr. Cain poured drinks. "To Cain-Taplin Limited," he said.

"Cheers," Pa replied.

I was about to rise up and stroll in as if I'd heard

nothing, when I heard Mr. Cain opening his cigar box. He offered Pa one, but he declined.

"Just think, Silas. It used to be against the law for a colored man to smoke a cigar or walk with a cane in the streets of Charleston. That's why we have to defeat these infernal codes. Someday, when he's a leading citizen of this town, Ezra should be able to stroll proudly through these streets with cane in hand, just like my cousin. Come to think of it, why doesn't Ezra use a cane?"

"He's never wanted one," Pa told him. He was right. I didn't even want to use a stick when I was just a tiny boy on the Stewart plantation. I didn't want to be different from the other kids, so I just kept up as best I could.

"Henry's noted that they have similar handicaps," said Mr. Cain. "If you like, I'm sure Henry could persuade his doctor to have a look at him."

"We'd be much obliged, but I don't suppose there's much he could do."

"Maybe. Maybe not. He was born that way, right?"

"No, not exactly," I thought I heard Pa say.

"Really? That's what he told me," Mr. Cain said.

"That's what he's been told," Pa said. *What I'd been told?* I sat up straight. Suddenly it was hard to breathe.

When Pa began to speak again his voice sounded far away, the way it always did when he talked about my mother, fingering her ragged dress while he watched her romp through his memories. This time was different, though. There was a sharp-edged anger to his speech. He gasped occasionally, as if choking back a sob.

"Most times it was tolerable on the Stewart plantation. The Missus was kind to us as she could be. She was softhearted and seemed to feel bad about our situation. Massa wasn't much worse unless he'd been drinkin', and once you'd been around him a while you could figure out how to handle him. But their son Judah, he was evil. I get religion like most folks. I go to the praise house and shout for God and ask for His mercy. Sometimes, though, I think I wouldn't mind being sent to Hell because I know I'd see Judah Stewart in the middle of all those fiery flames. That sight by itself would be worth eternal torment. Thaddeus, I apologize for blasphemin' in your house."

"Hush about that, man," Mr. Cain said. "Please continue."

"Massa Stewart was away on business. He left his son in charge. One day Judah come roaring out the house talking about his whiskey missin'. He stinkin' of liquor and ravin' about his favorite bottle. 'One of you musta stole it,' he say. He made all of us come out the fields and line up by the big house. I was stuck in the far field with a busted plow, so I was slow comin'. I was a foreman, so I got extra responsibilities. Massa Stewart knew I just couldn't come runnin' every time somebody drop a bottle. I took my time. Most everybody else was out there watchin' this man cry and carry on about his whiskey. The other foreman, the pickers, the trash gang, the baby mammy, the house servants, all lined up and lookin'. My Journee, she work in the house. She lined up too. Ezra a little bitty thing, ain't been around but for two harvests.

107

The mammy, her name was Emma, she was holdin' my boy in her arms.

"I decided to bring in the plow to see if it can be saved. I could see Judah struttin' around, but I couldn't really hear him. Not yet. I found out later that he was tryin' to make the house servants confess to stealin' his whiskey. Nobody confessed because nobody took it. Emma told me Judah reached out and snatched Ezra out of her arms.

" 'Somebody better tell me where my whiskey is,' he say, 'or this little whelp's gonna get it.' He held Ezra up so everybody could see him. Emma say he not cryin' or anything. Just lookin' around in wonder. I was in back of a shed now, got a whole building between me and Judah, so I couldn't see a thing. I bent over the plow then I heard a sound I still hear every night. It was the shrill cry of a wounded thing, full of pain and surprise like a bird shot out of the air. It's a baby, I think. A baby crying out. I straightened up, and a voice told me, 'Start runnin', Silas. Run as fast as you can.'

"Emma told me Judah just took Ezra's foot and twisted it and twisted it until it snapped. Ezra screamed and Journee hollered. I was halfway there and I saw my wife throwing herself at Judah. She so full of rage that it was pushing her through the air. Her arms outstretched, her fingers straining for Judah's throat. He was holding my baby like a rag doll, shaking him. His foot hanging there all wrong, like it was barely connected to his ankle. Judah tossed Ezra away and laughed. From the corner of my eye I saw Emma scoopin' up the baby. In front of me I saw

Judah swing his arm and slap my Journee to the ground."
Pa stopped for a second and tried to stifle his sobs. I
couldn't see him, but I knew tears were sliding silently
down his face. I knew because I was crying too.

"I hit Judah," Pa continued. "He was drunk. He went
down easy, curled up right away like he was sleep. It was
Luke that kept me from killing him. When Judah woke
up, he put me in the sweatbox 'til his daddy came back.
When I got out, Emma had Ezra. His foot was ruined,
and Judah said he'd kill anyone what tried to fix it. Emma
told me Journee's gone, took off running. Said she had to
run or else tear her hair out and lose what was left of her
mind. Emma said she tried to stop Journee but couldn't.
Journee told Emma that Ezra would always hate her for
not protecting him. Said I'd never forgive her for letting it
happen. But she was wrong. I never saw her again."

"Dreadful," Mr. Cain said somberly.

"Ever since, it's been just Ezra and me."

Outrage and wonder swept through me, making me
shiver. I stared down at my foot and blinked hard, as if
blinking would take back my father's words, take back my
whole sad history and leave me happy with a healthy foot
that worked. I'd never known that my mother had escaped
from slavery. Pa had always allowed me to believe that
she'd been sold away. No one at the Stewart plantation—
Luke, Clara, Emma—had ever dared to tell me the truth,
about either my foot or my mother. My head started
throbbing. Hot tears coursed down my cheeks. It was too
much information to take in at once. I wanted to cry and

shout at the same time. I was suddenly angry at the world, and especially Pa for keeping our terrible past a secret. I shoved the book off my lap, and it landed with a loud thump. I stood up and pushed the front door open. I slammed it behind me and limped away as fast as I could. I could hear Pa shouting my name behind me but I just pushed on faster, going nowhere in particular, just away.

But fast is not very fast at all when you've got a bum foot. My father caught me from behind, and I fought him hard, kicking him with my one good foot and pounding him with both fists. "Let me go!" I screamed. "You're a liar! You've lied to me all my life! I hate you!"

The world started spinning violently, making me feel sick to my stomach. Then everything went black.

I woke up in a room I didn't recognize. I felt strange, as if I was floating above the floor. I felt around with my hand. When it seemed to sink into the soft stuff surrounding me, I panicked and tried to sit up. A firm, feminine hand pushed me back.

"Relax, child," Miss Charlotte advised. "You're in a bed, that's all."

It was true. A big, wide bed supported by four mahogany posters. I'd seen beds before but had never lain in one. It felt too soft, like it could swallow me up until I disappeared forever. Miss Charlotte wiped my forehead with a cool cloth. Now, that felt good. I closed my eyes and breathed deeply as she went about her business, adjusting my pillow and bringing a cup of water to my lips. Savoring the faint scent of Miss Charlotte's perfume, I thought, this must be what it's like to have a mother. But as soon as that thought entered my mind it was followed by thoughts of Journee. How she ran away, and my father never told me. How Pa had lied to me all these years. I turned away from Miss Charlotte and bit my lip. Facing the window, I could hear the trundle of wagon wheels and the clip-clop of horses' hooves as the residents of Charleston headed home in the gathering dusk.

"You can't make your father wait forever," Miss Charlotte said.

"I don't see why not," I said. "He's used to waiting."

"You're almost a man, Ezra Taplin, but only almost. You still need your father. And he needs you."

"He doesn't need me. He likes being alone, being all sad-eyed when everyone else is happy, sitting up late with his memories and my mother's dress. If I ran away, I'd just leave behind a shirt or something. He prefers scraps of cloth to real people. They're easier to lie to." I was still facing the window. I didn't want her to see my tears if I started crying again. Hadn't she just said I was almost a man?

"You silly boy," Miss Charlotte said, clucking her tongue. "You're so caught up in your little-boy life that you miss most of what's going on right in front of you. You think everyone else is happy? Busy is what we are. Trying to make a future out of all this uncertainty. This town—and every town around here—is full of people looking for folks they've loved and lost. Sons, husbands, daughters, wives. Your Pa isn't the only one. You should know better than I because you help Thaddeus write the ads in his paper."

She was right. If he wanted to, Mr. Cain could have filled the entire *Colored Carolinian* with the same desperate words. Seeking information about Sarah, Cato, Samuel . . .

Miss Charlotte continued. "Sure, Silas is sad. We're all sad. But the world doesn't stop turning because of that, and we know it. And because we know it we keep working. Fighting. Farming. Teaching. Learning. And yes, mourning. But never sulking and never pouting. Because there's a difference. Your father knows the difference. Someday, if you're lucky, you will too."

I didn't say anything. I kept my back to her. Finally I heard her rise from her chair.

"I'm going to bring in your father," she said.

Pa came in almost as soon as Miss Charlotte left. I turned in his direction and kept my eyes half-closed, as if I was nearly asleep. I watched as he gingerly lowered himself into the chair next to the bed, as though he was afraid he might break it.

"Thaddeus has got himself one fine house," he began. "Back at the Stewarts' I used to wonder if colored people anywhere had big houses of their own. This isn't nearly as big as the Stewarts', but it's sho' grand all the same. That's what Missus used to call something she really admired. Grand."

When I said nothing, Pa kept on talking.

"Things go right, we'll have one of these ourselves. Not

a cabin, but a real home, with beds, not pallets made of corn shucks. . . . Thaddeus and I are going to be partners."

"I heard," I said. I kept my eyes half-closed.

"I think it might be a good thing for a boy who's going to be a writer to see what it's like having a bed, nice clothes, a room of his own."

I felt myself softening despite my best efforts to appear cross and unforgiving. I was imagining the things Pa described.

"Look, son, I know that's not all you heard. . . ."

"Why, Pa? Why didn't you tell me?"

"Life is hard enough, Ezra. I didn't want to make it any harder."

"You told me I was born crippled."

"Until now, all colored folks was born crippled."

"You know what I mean, Pa—my foot."

"I'm sorry about that, son. I didn't want you to grow up so bitter that you couldn't see your way through life. I did what I thought was best. I see now that I was wrong."

"What about my mother? All this time I thought she was sold away from you before you had a chance to say good-bye or find out where she was going. You never told me that she ran. She left me because I wasn't any good to her anymore, not as a cripple."

"You're wrong, Ezra," Pa said. His voice had been full of sorrow, but now it had an edge to it, a hint of anger. I opened my eyes and studied his face. "She left because she thought she wasn't any good to you anymore, because she couldn't save you."

I tried to picture my mama standing helplessly while

Judah Stewart held me in the air. I tried to feel what she felt watching her baby broken and twisted like a corn shuck doll. It was too much. I closed my eyes and bit my lip, but it didn't do any good. The tears came anyway. "She isn't coming back, Pa," I sniffed. "She's gone for good."

"Maybe you're right," Pa said softly. "But I got to keep on hopin'. Without hope, anger and sadness will use up all that's left of me. Won't be anything left for you. You and hope are all I got. I love you, Ezra."

I reached for Pa. He pulled me to him and squeezed me tight. The rough stubble of his face scratched my cheek as his large, callused hands rubbed my back. "I love you too," I said.

We held each other for a long time. Finally, Pa suggested that we head home. "We'd best get outta here before Thaddeus thinks we're movin' in."

I made a silent promise to my father. I swore to him that I would never again lose patience when he repeated some story from his past, such as the time he picked strawberries with Journee and he asked her to jump the broom—to be his wife—or the time a skunk sprayed them both and no one would go near them for days. No longer would I roll my eyes and suck my teeth when I woke up at night and found him at the table staring into empty space, rubbing Journee's dress down to the bare thread. But a strange thing happened. He stopped talking so much about my mother. In fact he hardly mentioned her at all. And he folded up the dress and put it away. More than two years passed before I saw it again.

Chapter 10

Our confrontation made Pa and me closer, although our relationship changed because of it. Because I had shown him that I could handle the truth, Pa no longer felt that he had to protect me all the time. He didn't send me on an errand anymore when men came by to talk to him. Instead he let me listen in and even offer an opinion—as long as I spoke respectfully. In time I began to make my own way in the world, and Pa showed a willingness to step aside while I took my first, halting steps.

Meanwhile, over the next two years Pa tasted prosperity for the first time. Despite his doubts, he slowly got used to the idea of being a landowner. With Henry Allen often acting as a go-between, Pa and Uncle Thaddeus (he'd encouraged me to stop calling him Mr. Cain) had expanded their holdings to 200 acres by the end of 1867. With his eye on Charleston's still-growing population, Pa concentrated on growing corn and vegetables—foodstuffs that would be eagerly grabbed by newcomers and tradesmen who moved straight into the city and had no plans to farm.

Pa hired more men to work the fields so that he could concentrate on his original dream of being a carpenter like Mose Bolton. Instead of shuffling from door to door in search of a roof to repair or shutters to make, Pa now had bigger plans. He intended to take over the building opportunities that became available in Robert Vesey's absence. Denmark's son had been an admired builder and gifted architect. Two years ago he'd overseen the construction of the new African Methodist Episcopal church. The old church had been burned down in the wake of his father's trial and execution. But he left town for good after completing the project, and there was still plenty of building to do. Silas Taplin believed he was the right man for the job. He began to recruit a crew from the carpentry class he was teaching on behalf of the Missionary Society.

Uncle Thaddeus had plans too. He'd convinced Oliver Walker to at least consider working with Cain-Taplin Limited to reopen the markets above the Cooper River. Once a bustling series of stalls operated by independent colored peddlers and fishmongers, the area had declined by the arrival of the Civil War. "If the South is going to rise again," Uncle Thaddeus had said with a laugh, "then so can those markets."

In April, Pa tested his crew—a mixture of newcomers

and seasoned hands who had worked with Robert Vesey—
by enlisting their aid in building a project on a plot of
ground on Blank Street, in the same neighborhood as
Uncle Thaddeus's place. Patience Walker and I stopped by
after school to watch the men make a foundation from
oyster shells and sand. Patience smiled when Pa bent low
and kissed her hand. He seemed happier than ever before,
giddy even.

"What's it going to be, Mr. Taplin?"

"Why, Miss Walker, I was hoping you'd ask me that.
This here is the future home of Silas and Ezra Taplin." Pa
looked at me and winked.

"Our own home, Pa? With a floor?"

Pa was laughing now. "Not just a floor, but beds too—
and glass windows."

Patience understood why I whooped with joy. She
already lived in such a house and knew the many pleasures
it provided.

Pa had Precious Walker sew him some new duds,
including a new pair of pants with extra pockets and loops
for holding tools. Folks took notice of the new look he
had about him, the way he walked with a bounce and
carried a gleam in his eye. Hiram Larkin told him that he
"shined like new money." We suspected that Uncle
Thaddeus had been pulling strings behind the scenes
when Zion Presbyterian asked Pa to join the Deacon
Board that June. But when we asked him about it, he just
threw up his hands and said, "The Lord works in
mysterious ways."

The Taplins weren't the only folks going through changes. Although I was only 13 myself, I was mature enough to recognize that Hiram had become a different man. His courtship of Malindy Johnson was clearly good for him. He didn't try to turn everything into a joke like he used to, and he wasn't as restless as before. Instead of fidgeting around while the other men talked about serious business, he now listened thoughtfully and even offered his own sensible opinions. He was still quick to smile and fun-loving but in a way that was charming instead of annoying. He and Malindy got married the first week of July.

I thought that watching the joyous couple walk down the aisle of Zion Presbyterian would put Pa in a sad mood, but luckily I was wrong. I guess he was too busy to let his mind wander to his own happier time.

The house was done in November, and we moved in right away. We had a celebration and invited Uncle Thaddeus, Miss Charlotte, Hiram and Malindy, and Oliver Walker and Prudence and Patience. (Mr. Walker's oldest daughter, Precious, had gotten tired of waiting for my father and married a minister from Philadelphia whom she'd known for most of her life.) The house had three bedrooms, a parlor, a kitchen, an outhouse in back, and a room that Pa would not let me in until all our guests had arrived. Finally, when Pa gave the signal, I turned the knob.

It was a library! The shelves, tall and sturdy, showed evidence of my father's skillful, loving hands. They were

empty except for a few books donated by Uncle Thaddeus
and Miss Charlotte. I grabbed a familiar volume and
opened it. Inside, in flowing script that I recognized at
once, was written "To Thaddeus, My Dear Friend and
Ally. Yours in the Cause of Liberty, Frederick Douglass."

"Just a little something to get your collection started,"
Uncle Thaddeus said. He was beaming from ear to ear.

"Thank you, thank you," I said, staring at the towering
shelves. I was looking forward to filling them, which
would probably take a lifetime. I continued to express my
gratitude to everyone there until finally Pa suggested that
we thank the Lord for a change, since He had provided
this wonderful home and the bountiful feast we were
about to enjoy.

"Thank you, Lord, for all the blessings we have
received since coming to Charleston," my father began.
We were all gathered around the polished oak table that
my father had made. "Thank you for our good friends and
our good fortune."

Most colored Carolinians still felt they had little to be
grateful for in 1867. The Fourteenth Amendment, which
guaranteed rights of citizenship to blacks, had passed the
year before, but it still needed to be ratified by the states in
order to become law. The amendment was part of
"Reconstruction," an effort to overcome the divisions
caused by the Civil War and reunite the nation. President
Andrew Johnson thought Reconstruction should involve
little more than punishing some of the rebellious
Southerners who had pushed for secession. According to

Uncle Thaddeus, the president just sat and watched while state governments across the South enacted Black Codes to keep former slaves in their place. In his editorials, Uncle Thaddeus praised Charles Sumner, Benjamin F. Wade, and other radical Republicans in Congress as "friends of our Cause." They were behind the Fourteenth Amendment and other measures meant to make us equal in the eyes of the law.

But many whites laughed openly at the idea of treating us as equals. Freedmen who knew nothing except picking cotton desperately agreed to sharecropping arrangements with the diehard "secesh" who owned the large plantations at Parker's Ferry and near Dorchester, just outside the city. In 1865 General William T. Sherman had issued "special field order no. 15," promising 40 acres and a mule to freed slaves. By midyear some 400,000 emancipated slaves had moved onto land under Sherman's jurisdiction, an area stretching from Charleston to the St. John's River in Florida. In March 1866 federal troops forced the blacks off the land—just as they had done on Edisto Island—and returned the property to its original owners. A year later it was clear to many that General Sherman's orders were little more than empty words.

In some quarters of colored Charleston, the spirit of Denmark Vesey was alive and well. Men like Mr. Walker and Uncle Thaddeus were seen by some as too patient and forgiving of the city's cruel past. A new group that would later call itself the Young Men's Progressive Association held meetings and discussed ways of improving life for freedmen. Uncle Thaddeus dutifully reported their activities in the *Colored Carolinian* and offered his editorial columns as a forum for their ideas.

The new spokesmen emerging from these groups had been pressed into action by the riots of the previous year, 1866. In Memphis a mob of whites went on a rampage through the city's colored quarter, killing 46 blacks and stealing or destroying more than $130,000 worth of property, all of it owned by blacks. That summer, Mr. Cain had congratulated me on turning 12 while we prepared another issue of the paper. We were carrying a report on the New Orleans riot, which had just taken place in July amid the growing popularity of the Klan, the group that had begun in Tennessee. Thirty-four blacks had been killed in New Orleans. I remembered the words of the old man from Arkansas who had come to the Colored People's Convention. "They ride by night, and we die by day," he had warned, but he was only half right. The Klan in New Orleans was riding by day *and* night.

We got our first look at the South Carolina Klan shortly after we moved into the new house. The sound of yelling, excited voices drew us to the window not long after dark. Pa and I got there in time to see a group of torch-bearing night riders thundering through the streets. They were all dressed in bed sheets, and hoods covered their faces. "Bring us the head of Telemaque," the rider in front shouted. "We're looking for Telemaque!" The other riders clanked chains and made moaning and wailing sounds, as if they were ghosts out on a moonlit hant.

In his passionate letters and editorials, Telemaque continued to anger both whites and blacks as he argued for increased rights for the nation's freedmen and women. He criticized blacks for being too timid and attacked whites as greedy, unfair, and unwilling to share the country's wealth—wealth, he pointed out, that was built on the backs of slaves. In a recent editorial he had pointed out the similarities between sharecropping and slavery. "Four hundred thousand people who were slaves before the war do not even now own their labor. Their labor is owned by the landowner who controls and directs it," he wrote.

Telemaque and Pa shared similar ideas about land ownership. Like my father, Telemaque often observed that God wasn't making any more land. He urged blacks to get as much of it as they could, a point of view that Pa was gradually beginning to understand. Telemaque was far more outspoken than Pa, though, and loved to sound off about anything that was on his mind. He wasn't exactly secretive about his opinions.

But he was secretive about his identity. "Telemaque" was a pen name. No one knew who he really was. Uncle Thaddeus claimed not to know, although some suspected that he himself was Telemaque. Hiram and others had pointed out that Telemaque's letters were written in a eloquent, logical style, as if their author had read many law books.

Telemaque had enraged local whites by writing a new pamphlet offering a plan to put more land into the hands of blacks. The pamphlet, which the new improvement association made available at its meetings, suggested that the state purchase 80,000 homesteads of 10 acres each for the freedmen and women. Under his plan the homesteaders would have four years to pay back the state. After paying for their farms, the new owners would make improvements that would surely "enhance the valuation and price of the lands in all parts of the state."

The Klan had had enough of colored boys trying to tell white folks what to do. Somebody needed to be taught a lesson. As we watched the night riders rush by, Pa and I had the same thought: Uncle Thaddeus.

"You stay here," Pa said, but I grabbed him by the shoulder.

"You can't beat them on foot, Pa. Besides, I want to go with you."

Pa looked at me a minute; then he reached out and gently stroked my cheek. It surprised me. "All right, son. But let me go on ahead. You catch up when you can. And be careful."

He quietly stepped out of the house, looked left and right, and then trotted off, keeping to shadows made by the oaks lining the avenue. I waited a minute before taking off myself. It was slow going for me in the dark. Although there was moonlight, I still had to step carefully to avoid ruining my already-damaged ankle. By the time I limped around the corner of Bull Street, the worst had already happened.

Mr. Cain lay in a pool of blood. Pa was cradling Mr. Cain's head in his hands. The night riders had already gone. "They wanted Telemaque," Mr. Cain gasped.

"Shh," Pa whispered. "Don't talk."

"I told them Telemaque was a figment of their

123

imagination, the black angel of their dreams." Mr. Cain tried to laugh but choked instead. Blood dripped from his lips. "Shh," Pa said again. "Hush and lie still."

That night Hiram showed up with the wagon, and we drove Mr. Cain to our house. Fussed over and attended to by Miss Charlotte and Prudence Walker, he gradually recovered. The Klan continued to attack and terrorize here and there, so far unsuccessful in their attempt to locate and punish the fearless Telemaque.

By the winter of 1867 Uncle Thaddeus was back to his hearty, bigger-than-life self. That Christmas he asked Pa to stand up for him at his wedding to Miss Charlotte Wells. He told Pa, "One day I was lying there in pain, and Charlotte reached over and touched my hand. Just like that the pain was gone. I thought the absence of pain was the release you feel before going to Glory. I said to her, 'I don't want to die without asking you to marry me.' She said, 'You're not going to die this night. I won't allow you to.'"

The newlyweds spent the first months of the new year in Philadelphia, visiting friends and renewing old acquaintances. I filled in for Miss Charlotte at the school, taking the youngsters through the alphabet, reading them stories aloud, writing out the numbers on a big black slate. I took some advertisements for Uncle Thaddeus too. Although Pa hardly ever mentioned it anymore, a certain ad still ran in every issue. "Information Wanted of Journee Taplin," it began, "last seen in Orange County, North Carolina, in 1856. . . ."

Chapter 11

My favorite memory of freedom begins with a simple sound. The distant trundle of wagon wheels growing deeper and louder as a wagon approaches. I'm at the far end of Blank Street, nearly a block from my home. It's spring 1869, and I've got a ball made of rolled-up rags—tossing it high in the air, catching it as it comes tumbling down.

It's early in the morning and fairly quiet, so the sound of the trundling wheels travels all the way up the block and easily reaches my ear. I turn and see the wagon. I see my father coming outside to greet the driver. Wagons come to our house all the time. I turn away and toss my ball again. Somehow I miss it when it comes tumbling down. I bend over to pick it up, and a sensation comes over me that I can't explain. Suddenly I hear Pa's voice saying, "When we're really, truly free, somehow we'll know it." I'm dizzy for a second, as though I'm on a ship rocked by a raging storm. Then suddenly I'm on solid ground, and the whole world looks strangely clean, so bright and shiny that it sparkles. I have to squint to avoid being dazzled by the light.

I'm standing there holding that ball, staring at it but not seeing it—when something tells me, "Run, Ezra. Run as fast you can."

Except with a foot like mine you don't really run. In fact, you just shuffle and hop. But I'm running—so swift and so well that I wonder if I'm dreaming, but I can't be because I can feel the ground under my feet and the air moving through my lungs, and I'm almost flying when I see my father lift a woman in his arms, so high her feet leave the ground. He's squeezing her and crying and bawling into her neck. "Journee. My Journee," he says.

And all of a sudden she stops. She feels my eyes on her, and she turns to me and I see a face just like mine staring back at me. I see that face go from joy to shock to fear to joy again as I fling my arms wide, and we are three together, hugging, kissing, babbling, not letting go. I think my Pa is right: We are really, truly free. And we know it.

This painting shows Abraham Lincoln with his cabinet, assembled for a first reading of the Emancipation Proclamation on July 22, 1862. The proclamation took effect on January 1, 1863.

Officers and men of the 39th U. S. Colored Infantry, 1864

American abolitionist and writer Frederick Douglass

Ruins in Charleston, South Carolina, 1865

This illustration from *Harper's Weekly* was titled "Among the ruins of Columbia, South Carolina," 1866.